Doctors Scientists and Engineers of Ancient India

Doctors Scientists and Engineers of Ancient India

S. NARAIN

with a foreword by

Prof. P.B. Sharma

Founder Vice-Chancellor

Rajiv Gandhi Technological University

Bhopal

KALPAZ

ISBN: 978-93-5128-257-0

Price: ₹ 790

First Published, 2017

Published by

Kalpaz Publications
C-30, Satyawati Nagar,
Delhi – 110052
E-mail: kalpaz@hotmail.com
Ph.: 9212142040

Printed at: G. Print Process, Delhi

Cataloging in Publication Data—DK
Courtesy: D.K. Agencies (P) Ltd. <docinfo@dkagencies.com>

Narain, S., author.
Doctors, scientists and engineers of ancient India / S. Narain; with a foreword by Prof. P.B. Sharma.
pages cm
Includes bibliographical references.

1. Science—India—History. 2. Technology—India—History. 3. Medicine—India—History. 4. Physicians—India—History. 5. Scientists—India—History. 6. Engineers—India—History. I. Title.

Q127.I4N37 2016 DDC 509.54 23

Tel. : 011-27871018
Fax : 91-11-2787102

दिल्ली इन्जीनियरिंग कॉलेज
(राष्ट्रीय राजधानी क्षेत्र दिल्ली सरकार)

DELHI COLLEGE OF ENGINEERING
(Govt. of National Capital Territory of Delhi)

सत्यमेव जयते

Prof. P.B. SHARMA
Ph.d. (B'ham, U.K.)
FIE, FAeroS, FWAPS

बवाना रोड, दिल्ली - 110 042
Bawana Road, Delhi - 110 042

E-mail : pbsharma@dce.edu

FOREWARD

The treasure of science and technology in ancient India unfolds the wonder that was India; a scientifically advanced, technologically sound, materially prosperous and above all a spiritually enlightened India. It is now aboundantly clear that ancient India has surpassed all imaginations for the advancement of human kind in all the spheres of human endeavour which include art and architecture, town planning, development of human languages, musical nodes and compositions, literally writings, decimal system of counting, rapid computations using micro mathematical *sutras*, natural medicines, systems of governance and above all, a profound understanding of rhythms and virbations of nature and the intricate relationship between man, nature and the universe system. This treasure of ancient India, if sincerely and honestly deciphered, shall not only help us to understand and appreciate the magnificant heights of scientific and technological advancement in ancient India but shall also provide the much needed impetus to take the modern age of Information Technology driven developments to the unprecedented levels of wisdom propelled systems of tomorrow. The journey would then go on from present age of Information Technology, IT, to Knowledge Technolgoy, KT and then ultimately to Wisdom Technology, WT, *Gyana*, the knowledge, shall then transcened to *pragyana*, the wisdom multifold. The summit of life with divine would then become a reality in one's own life time as professed by Shri Aurbindo in his works on Life Divine.

A sincere and systematic attempt in this direction has been made by Shri S. Narain in his treatise on Ancient Scientists & Engineers". Shri Narain has drawn his inspiration for this book from his earlier work on Science & Technology in Ancient India, published some years ago while he was with us as Officer on Special Duty in Delhi College of Engineering. I am indeed happy to note that in the present work Shri Narain has elucidated the novel cause of scientific advancement in ancient India pursued by ancient India's scientists and technologists, wherein the scientists and engineers both worked relentessly for the development of a human society with scientific temper and technological acumen.

Shri Narain has traversed the journey of science and technology developments in ancient India from the early Vedic times to the times of Varahmihir, Aryabhatha, and Bhaskaracharya of the post Gupta's period. While Kanada, the founder of atomic theory in ancient India, from where the missiles, bombs and canons of Mahabharata were derived, the ancient system of medicines owes its profound origin in the works of Bhardwaja, Attreya, Charaka and Susurta, the Father of Surgery in ancient India. The material science genius of ancient India finds its fullest manifestation in the purity of wrought iron in the famous Iron Pillar in the Qutub Minar complex. The Nagarjuna of the ancient India and the successive clan of ancient India's great metallurgists made it possible to produce both the purified metals as well as composites which have received wide recognition and admistation from the modern materials scientists around the world. The great Buddha statue made of mixed metals weighing several tons and having a magnificent height, so tall that it could not be taken inside the Victoria Albert Museum in London are some of the testimony of the levels of prefection attained by ancient India's metallurgists. The decimal system of counting and the great mathematical treatises of Varahmihir and Aryabhata are still the source of inspiration for the development of faster computing and for ever increasing interest in quantum mechanics and space sciences.

The present teastise on Ancient India provides an in-depth insight into the treasure of science and technology in ancient India. I am sure while it shall inspire the younger generation of scientists and technologists around the world, it shall also lead to a new horizon for discovering its relevance to our quest for the development of a knowledge society. This publication in my opinion shall be a highly useful reference in the libraries of schools, colleges and universities in India and abroad. I wish the publication all success.

PROF. P.B. SHARMA
Principal & Dean (Faculty of Technology)
Delhi College of Engineering,
University of Delhi
also
Founder Vice-Chancellor
Rajiv Gandhi Technological University, Bhopal

December 3, 2004

PREFACE

India has a glorious past and is the heir of one of the most intellectual and spiritual traditions of the world. However, little is known about the foundation and development of science and technology and the scientists behind this progress in ancient India.

Throughout the long centuries of ancient India's history, the development of science and technology had been taking place, right from the times when the hymns of RigVeda were being composed. The foundation of Algebra was laid, the science of three angular characteristics - the trignometry, the science of astronomy medicine, surgery, vetenary, and even metallurgy took birth, developed and reached a high level of advancement besides discovering zero, the fundamental abstract of all sciences. This has been achieved due to the genius of ancient scientists and technologists of India. However no adequate light has been shed on the subject, spelling out the parallels between modern sciences and Indian wisdom.

The book aims to focus on the salient features of technological development and the founders of science who shared the full credit on this phenomenal progress enviable to western countries.

I am grateful to Prof. P.B. Sharma, founder Vice Chancellor, Rajeev Gandhi Technological University, Bhopal M.P. for his Forward note of the book.

S. Narain

CONTENTS

1

The Wonder that was India

1
THE WONDER THAT WAS INDIA

Ancient India has been, no doubt, the land of wonders and many a firsts. It is here in this country that a systematic and a formal attempt to understand the human speech, the swaras, the varnas and the matras, has been made several thousand years ago while the man in most of the countries was not even able to formally decipher his communication styles and skills. The languages have taken birth here, the grammar has been written here well before any where else, the numerals were discovered, the arithmetic, the beejganit, the geometry, the art and science of three angular characteristics, the trigonometry and the entire horizon of mathematical domain of the cosmos was very well comprehended by our ancestors well before the most of the other countries could grasp the enormous power of mathematics.

A civilization, which has such a sound mathematical base, has naturally to pursue science and engineering for improving the quality of life of its people and for the growth of wealth and prosperity of people of the world. It is surprising to know that the foundation of the laws of the thermodynamics[1] were laid here, the bio-chemistry and the quantum physics were well understood and this provided our ancestors a conviction in the eternal existence of man both in its matter and the energy. The vedic concept of Purna, the eternal, is born out of this conviction.

In fact, the entire material and spiritual development in India, from the ancient times to date, has been nurtured through a deep understanding of human existence in harmony with nature. We have gone far beyond the European concept of humanism (Manav Vad) to encompass in our fold all beings through our clear-cut emphasis on the welfare of one and all, 'Sarve Bhavantu Sukhina'[2]. There were not mere proclamations rather a commitment in word, deed and action of our ancestors who brought glory to this land of karma through their unconditional commitment to the cause of human upliftment.[2a]

TECHNOLOGICAL ADVANCEMENT

The height of technological advancement in ancient India is well manifested in the fabrication of aeroplane. Possession of aeroplane by Ravana, in epic period which was later on

1. ॐ पूर्णमदः पूर्णमिदं पूर्णात् पूर्णमुदच्यते।
   पूर्णस्य पूर्णमादाय पूर्णमेवावशिष्यते॥ *— Isa upnishad 1-1*
   This may be enterprated as the foundation of first law of thermodynamics; as 'Purna' stands for eternity of matter and the energy.
2. सर्वे भवन्तु सुखिनः सर्वे सन्तु निरामयाः।
   सर्वे भद्राणि पश्यन्तु मा कश्चिवद्दुःखभाग्भवेत्॥

2a. **Engineers of Tomorrow - Prepare to Compete Globally, Principal Prof. P.B. Sharma's Address to Freshers, Delhi College of Enigneering, August, 1994.**

used by Lord Rama for performing journey from Lanka to Ayodhya may not be a figment of imagination and is coming true in wake of[3] discovery of a manuscript, Vamanic Parkarnan, believed to have been authored by Rishi Bhardwaja, provides a valuable information in this regard. The script contains the methods and technology of fabricating aeroplane with the kind of tools and equipments available in those days. The conception and fundamentals, on which the fabrication of aeroplane is based, are entirely new and efforts are being made to decipher the script (See Hindustan Times dated 25.2.91).

ADVANCEMENT IN METALLURGY

Iron Pillar at Delhi

The metallurgical genius of India are well evident in the fabrication of wrought iron Pillar installed at Delhi which is still rust less even passing thousands of years without any effect of wind, rain, storm, hail etc. *Fa-hsien*, a famous Chinese *traveller* even saw an over 25 metre high image

---

3. एवमुक्तस्तु रामेण राक्षसेन्द्रो विभीषणः।
विमानं सूर्यसंकाशमाजुहाव त्वरान्वितः॥23॥
ततः काश्चनश्चित्राङ्ग वैदूर्यमणिवेदिकम्।
कूटागारः परिक्षिप्तं सर्वतो रजतप्रभम्॥24॥

— ***Ramayana by Valmiki Yudh Kanda p. 657***

of Buddha made of copper which is a landmark proving the advancement of metallurgy in ancient India. The Indian steel was exported to many countries of the world since very early and came to be called 'wootz' in later times. No other country in the world could manufacture such steel swords as were made by Indian technicians. They were in great demand in the entire region from Asia to Europe. In fact, the science and technology of metallurgy reached at highest pitch in ancient India. Nagarjuna, a philosopher, scientist and a metallurgist, par excellence in Gupta age was perhaps capable, according to Hiuen-Tsang, to convert stone into gold though appears impossible.

SCULPTURE AND ARCHITECTURE

The post Buddhist sculpture and stone work is an unparalleled marvel even at today's standard. V. Smith, a noted art Historian in his work 'Fine Art', observes with regard to the monolithic shaft of Ashoka Pillar as under :

"The fabrication, conveyance and erection of monoliths of such enormous size, the heaviest weighing about 50 tonnes are the proofs that the engineers and stone-cutters of Ashoka Age were not inferior in skill and resource to those of any time of country".

In fact, the stone technologists of ancient India during medieval period amazed the Muslim ruler Mahmud Gazani also who carried off these technicians to build at Gazani, Speaking about the magnificent monuments of Samarqand and the erection of the Sargin (stone) Mosque near the Iron Gate, Babar says that 'a number of stone-cutters were brought from Hindustan to work on it'.[4]

Capital of Ashokan Pillar, Sarnath (Near Benaras)

MATHEMATICS AND ASTRONOMY

The works of ancient Indian scientists were translated in Arabic and Persian particularly in mathematics and astronomy Arya Bhatta and Bhaskara are the most shining stars of ancient India in this regard. In fact India earned the distinction of many a firsts in mathematics. The place value system was for the first time used by India which was later on adopted by Arabs who spread it in western world. The Indian numerals appeared in the west centuries after. The decimal system on which the mathematics is based was used in India for the first time. The famous mathematician Arya Bhatta (AD 476-500) was acquainted with it. The Chinese, the Arabs all borrowed directly or indirectly from India. The distinction of discovery of Zero. treating it a separate numeral also goes to India in 2nd century BC where as Arabs who spread it to western Europe borrowed the knowledge from India several centuries after. The Hindu scientists and physicians were invited in foreign countries to install. them as chief physicians of their hospitals and the famous books on various sciences i.e. pharmacology, toxicology on snakes veterinary and veterinary sciences etc. were got translated from Sanskrit to Arabic etc. A Syrian astronomer of seventh century A.D. writes:

> *"No word can praise strongly enough the knowledge of the Hindus. If these things are known to the people who think that they alone have mastered the sciences because they speak Greek, they would perhaps be convinced though a little late in the day that other folk not only Greeks, but men of different tongue, know something as well as they".*

This all speaks volume about the proficiency attained by us in art, science & technology which can only be conjectured by the works which have left behind and the skill and refinement with which they are designed and constructed. The most marvellous monuments of the age, the dexterity as well as the delicacy displayed in the manufacture of woollen, silken and cotton fabrics, the height of workmanship shown in the technical treatment of wood, metal and stone; the astounding technique of dress and ornaments; and the constructive enactness

4. **Ershine's - Memories of Babar Vol. II, pp. 78-79.**

manifested in preparing the products of peace as well as the weapon of war -give one a fat idea of the kind of technology and the quality of technical training and vocational knowledge imparted in those days.

UNIVERSITY OF TAXILA

The university of Taxila was the most renowned seat of learning for many centuries in the East, especially for medicine and surgery[5] and it attracted students from far and near. The upsurge of pity and compassion for the unfortunate, the diseased and the disabled associated with the pity of Buddhism led to the multiplication of animal shelters and hospitals in the country.

Fa Hien (A.D. 4-5) makes the following observations concerning hospitals in the city of Pataliputra. "*The nobles and house holders have founded hospitals within the city to which the poor of all countries, the destitute crippled and diseased may repair. They receive every kind of requisite help gratuitously. Physicians inspect their diseases and according to their cases, order them food and drink, medicine and decoctions, everything in fact which may*

---

5. **Jataka 252, 356, 219, 415, 871**
   Jatakas several hundreds in number contain more than 500 stories of previous births of Gautam Budha as it is believed according to Buddhist doctrine that even the great Buddha had to pass through 84000 previous lives before he could become a Buddha, Many of the stories described in Jatakas are quite old and depict common life of ancient India and its economic and social conditions.

contribute to their ease. When cured they depart at their convenience".

NALANDA UNIVERSITY

The Nalanda University was the crest jewel of the educational institutions in the whole Asia and was embodiment of high ideal of education. Here foreign students from distant countries like China, Korea, Tibet came to study and to achieve fame as scholars. The highest academic degree or distinction of the times was the fellowship of Nalanda. Hiuen T Sang mentions.[6]

> *"Those who stole the name of Nalanda brother were all treated with respect wherever, they went and it was not mean and easy matter to obtain admission to Nalanda. The doors of the university were generously guarded by the specialist in the subject.*

---

6. **Biblography-Hiuen-T Sang (Beal's Translation)**
7. **Op.cit.**

NALANDA

No. 1 - Bird's-eye view of Monasteries, showing cells with verandah, courtyard, well and shrine

"Hiuen Tsang testifies". Those from abroad who wished to enter the schools of discussion, the majority beaten by the difficulties of the problems withdrew, and those who were deeply versed in old and modern learning were admitted only two or three out of ten succeeding".

The academic life was at a very high level both on its intellectual and its moral side. The students were looked up to as models all over India. The picture of academic life as drawn by Hiuen T sang as under:[7]

"In the establishment were some thousands of Brethen all men of great ability and learning, several hundreds being highly esteemed and famous; learning and discussing they found the day time short; day and night they admonished each other, juniors and seniors mutually helping of perfection".

FOREIGN INVASIONS

With the advent of Muslims in this country and their strong grip on most of India, the scenario underwent a change. The ancient learning and sciences were discarded and discouraged. The native technicians were looked down with suspicion. Master craftsmen were brought from Persia and other Muslim countries and Shiraj - a famous city, was taken as model in regard to education.

---

7. **Biblography-Hiuen-T Siang (Beal's Translation)**

The spate of foreign invasion burst upon this country, bigotry of Hindu society coupled with negative attitude of Muslim rulers in medieval times left most of ancient sciences nothing but the scanty remains of bygone better times as testified by Alberuni -a famous Arab traveller and scholar .

> ***"Mahmud utterly ruined the prosperity of the country and performed there wonderful exploits by which the Hindus became atoms of dust scattered in all directions and like a tale of old. This is the reason why Hindu sciences have retired far away from those parts of the country conquered by us and have fled to places where our hand yet cannot reach".***

2

Growth and Development of Various Sciences and Technology

2

GROWTH AND DEVELOPMENT OF VARIOUS SCIENCES AND TECHNOLOGY

'Necessity is the mother of Invention', this would apply to the growth of various sciences in every civilization including that India. Man's quest to solve the common problems of life and also to give answer to various necessities coming across, led to various discoveries which though appear small to a present man but were very important in those days.

Imagine the life without fire. No bread to eat, no cooked vegetables, no boiled rice, milk is also cool and raw, no cream is formed, neither any butter nor cheese. Also, in winter weather one would not have warm water to bath. Discovery of Fire was, therefore, a great achievement in those days.

Yajnas i.e. Fire sacrifice played an important part in the growth and development of various sciences in ancient India and the whole culture & civilization of this land developed around Yajnas in vedic age which is considered to be the dawn of Aryan civilization and Yajnas became an open laboratory as also observatory. The fire altars were constructed for performing Yajnas which were mainly of two types. The ones that were performed daily (nitya) and the other that were performed to achieve a particular objective (Kamya). Each sacrifice required a specific altar for it. Special shapes like falcon with spread wings, tortoise, birds, chariot wheel were given to the altars for performing Yajnas on special occasions.

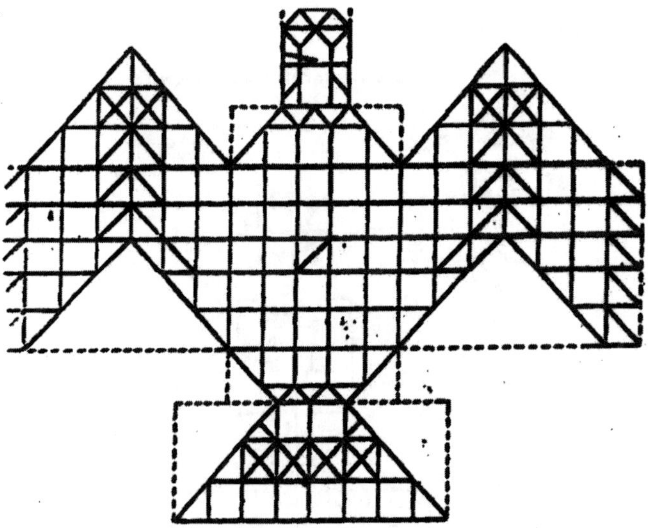

Fig. 1. : Altar with a falcon like shape.

The construction of these altars was a technology in itself and required knowledge of site preparation, demarcation of ground for altars, laying the bricks in several layers giving a particular shape to the altars and providing a good finishing. The technology like brick making developed. The site preparation for altars required the knowledge of civil engineering, construction engineering as well as architecture. Infact Brahman Satpatha an ancient literature of Vedic time contains details of the construction of such altars. Similarly, Baudhyana - a work of 800 B.C. mentions many a geometrical shapes for altars.

Layout of Altars

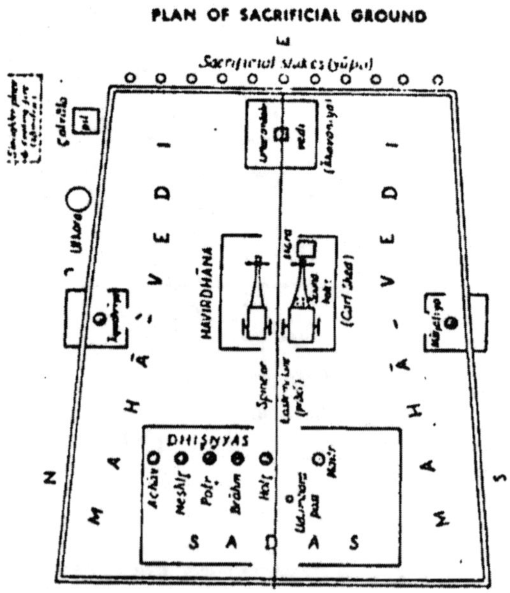

Fig. 2

The layout of the proper shape on the ground for the fire altar was also a job requiring an expert knowledge of the same as will be seen from the layout of fire altar of (Mahavedi), as has been described in Satapatha Brahmana in connection with Soma sacrifice. The great altar is an isosceles trapezium with base as 30 padas and altitude as 36 padas.

A chrmological account of development of various sciences is given as under :

MEDICAL SCIENCE

Medical science in ancient India is as old as Rigveda as transpires from the hymn ix-112.

Fig. 3

"We different men have different aptitudes and pursuits. The carpenter deals with broken things, the physician a patient, the priest some one who will perform sacrifice."

No doubt an ailing person craves for medical treatment as such medicines form an intergral part of any human civilization and therefore, it is no wonder that major part of Atharv Veda is devoted to the treatment of various diseases such as fever, jaundice and other disorders. Even the Rigveda, considered to be most ancient work of Aryan civilization mentions the name of one thousand and one medicinal herbs.[1] The physicians had to go out into the open streets, calling out for patients.[2] They lived in houses surrounded by gardens of medicinal herbs. The rudiments of embryology, midwifery, child management (padiatrics) and sanitation were formulated in the age of the Vedas and Brahmanas.

In vedic period, the medical science practitioners were divided as:

(i) Physician (Bhisaka).
(ii) Salya Vaidya (Surgeon).
(iii) Bhisagatharvan (Priest doctors).

Whereas Mahabharta mentions the five branches by adding poison curers (visaharas) and Damon doctors (Krlyaharas) as the separate specialization.

---

1. तक्षा रिष्टं रुतं भिषक् - Rv. IX. 112.1
2. शतं वो अम्ब धामानि सहस्रमुत वो रुहः। - Rv. X. 97.2
शतं ते राजन् भिषजः सहस्रमुर्वी गभीरा सुमतिष्ठे अस्तु। - Rv. I. 24.9

The development of medical science is attributed to the following Rishis:

(i) Dhanvantri (ii) Bhardwaja (iii) Attreya

Medical science developed considerably later on into following branches by 100 B.C.

(i) Surgery
(ii) Midwifery
(iii) Mental diseases
(iv) Diseases of eye, nose, ear etc.
(v) Practice of medicine
(vi) Paediatrics
(vii) Aphrodisiac.

During the glorious reign of Emperor Ashoka, hospitals. were opened for animals and men alike. Medicinal drugs were planted and supplied according to needs.

During the Buddhist period, we are fortunate to get an additional light thrown on the condition of this profession. The Vinay contains information regarding several ailments and the medicines (chiefly herbs) administered to cure them. The use of a variety of medicinal oils is also referred to. There is evidence of the use of surgical instruments as well.

As per Mahauagga, Taxila must have been the most renowned seat of medical education in the country. It attracted students from such a distant part of the country as Rajagahaod.

The course of medical studies then extended to a period of seven years, after which a practical examination was held, putting to the test the student's knowledge of medical botany or his first-hand acquaintance with the medicinal plants and their properties.

In case of surgery, difficult operations were successfully carried out as those upon the skull, or the belly to set right twisted intestines.

We are much obliged to Susruta who through his work Susruta-Samhita systematically compiled the surgical experiences of old dethroned and tied together the scattered facts of the science from the vast volume of Vedic literature.

As per Charaka, no one can obtain complete mastery in all branches of the Ayurveda. But mastering merely one branch was also not enough because no single. branch of the Ayurveda was spread over its all branches,. has been suggested viz,: (i) Physicians, (ii) Surgeons, (iii) Druggists, (iv) Mid-wifery, (v) Nursing, (vi) Veterinary Surgeons, (vii) Preservers of corpses, etc. The absence of unanimity of opinion in regard to the specialized branches of medical practice does not however obscure the fact of its advanced stage of development. Indeed, it confirms it. Besides Susruta and Charaka, a medico-botanical glossary called Nighantu was also then in existence.

HOW THE MEDICAL EDUCATION WAS IMPARTED

Eligibility for Admission : Admission to medical education was not granted indiscriminately. Only those who had requisite intelligence, physically fit with well formed organs such as tongue, lips, teeth, eyes, nose and mouth, good manners, patience and courage, and cheerful look were admitted for imparting education as transpires from Susruta Samhita where it has also been laid down that a physician ought to be resourceful, experienced, truthful and cheerful. This shows that while granting student ship the Acharya would satisfy himself in regard to possessing these qualities by the aspirant student. The underlying idea is very much valid as the practicing physician should himself be of healthy mind and healthy body and be a man of strict morale as he would treat all sorts of patients under all conditions.

Probation Period : As per evidence of Susrut samhita, the admission granted to a student was provisional and the student would be deemed on probation for six months to ensure the fitness of the admitted student for study of medical science.[3]

Upanayana Ceremony : Admission for study of medical science was formalized through a ceremony called upanayana which could be performed on an auspicious day.

The course of medical studies was 7 years or more after which an examination was held to ensure that the student had

3. Ashtauga Haridya Sutra Sthana Ch.II.

the requisite knowledge and skill in medical science[4] as per evidence of Mahavagga, there was considerable progress in surgery and some difficult operations were also done. The example of Zivaka shows that surgery in regard to skull and belly setting right the twisted intestines were done. A huge fee for treating dangerous disease was charged as transpires from the story of Zivaka.

Method of Study : The study of medical science/ Ayurveda commenced from padas and Shalokas which were to be committed to memory with their meaning well understood. It was stressed upon to learn the import as well, without which he was compared to a donkey bearing the burden of sandal wood without enjoying its fragrance.[5]

A medical student was enjoined to acquire a double proficiency in both theory and practice like the two wheels of a chariot to move and to perform its functions. A physician if only a theoretician and devoid of surgical skill has been compared to a murderer killing the patients under the licence of the King. Similarly a medical practitioner without theoretical knowledge of medical science deserves to be penalized by the King because even the amrit will act as poison if applied wrongly and in sheer ignorance.

---

4. Susruta. Sanhita Ch. II.
5. Susruta Ch. II

Award of Licence : After completing the course of study a student of medical science was awarded a licence to practice by the King.

MILITARY SCIENCE

Aryans had to fight several battles to establish themselves and to spread their civilization necessitating war fare for a long period. There is mention of forts in Rigveda and also numerous instances in other Vedas to this effect. Rigveda[6] refers to the blockade of 100 cities of non Aryana by Rijasvan in his fight against 'Krishna Garbhan means dusky complexioned people.

Similarly, Rigveda iv, 30.21 mentions like killing of 30,000 Dasas.

Fig. 4

6. Rigveda i, 53,8.

In another passage of Rigveda (X, 22,8) there is a prayer to Indra "destroyer of foes kill them. Destroy the Dasa race". We are surrounded on all sides by Dasyu tribe.

Military Science made a considerable progress during the Epic period where it was exalted to the status of an upveda and the term Dhanurveda encompassed the entire military science and art of the age and it conveyed different kinds of military knowledge and accomplishment. The skill of seizing of weapons and the arts of discharging weapons simultaneously, act of advancing and retreating etc.. In other words the entire contents of practical skill and knowledge of military education were included under the term of Dhanurveda comprising of following:[7]

(i) Club fighting.
(ii) Sword wielding
(iii) Archery
(iv) Spear throwing
(v) Fighting with missiles.
(v) Seizing weapons
(vi) Rathsiksha i.e. the skill whereby the warior learn the art of circling with his war car of doubling and returning the skill of avoiding being made a viratha (deprived of one's war car) and preventing it from being splintered into fragments by the attack of the enemy.

The Military science also comprised of organizing of: (i) Patrols (ii) Battalian (iii) Army as per evidence of Mahabharta.

7. Mahabharta Sastragrahan Vidya vi. 76.7, 4.8 vii. 23,29

Military Schools : Instances are not lacking to the functioning of schools of military education in ancient India. Patanjali mentioned such schools in his Mahabhasya. Similarly in Taxila University a school of Archery was famous for training in the skill where more than a hundred princes studied.

Mahabharta mentions as under the military valour of Abhimanyu (son of Arjuna)

"The powerful boy became equal to his father in counteracting the weapons hurled upon him in great lightness of hand, in fleetness of motion forward and backward and in traversing and wheeling".

Fig. 5

The formal admission to military education was done through a ceremony called Upanayana as per reference of Vashistha. The ceremony comprised of giving a weapon to the military students and vedic mantras were recited by the teacher who was supposed to be accomplished in the use of the seven weapons as under:

(i)	Bow	(ii)	Disc
(iii)	The sword	(iv)	The spear
(v)	The mace	(vi)	The arms
(vii)	The Kharikara		

The weapon to be held by the students in the Upanayana ceremony would be different for different caste, a brahman student - a bow, a kshatriya student -a sword, for vaisya -a lance and for a sudra - a mace.

Graduate in Military science as cited in Viramtrodhya the completion of military training was marked by a ceremony called (Chhurika bandhnan) and comprised of tying a dagger to the dress of the student supposed to be the graduate in military science.

Industrial Art and Technology

In ancient India, every craft man with his house as workshop was an industry unto himself. The various articles including of domestic and industrial use were turned out by him manually in the workshop. The workshop was acting as a training school for the aspirant pupil who may be a son, relatives or an apprentice. The crafts which were in practice during vedic/ later vedic period were as under:

Industrial Occupations:

1. Smith
2. Smelter
3. One who makes arrows.
4 Potter.
5. Bow-maker
6. Carpenter
7. Stone-Carver
8. Carver
9. Basket-maker
10. Dyer
11. Goldsmith
12. Weaver
13. Female weaver
14. A female embroiderer
15. Chariot-Builder
16. Rope maker
17. Wine-Distroiller

The number of these crafts went up considerably later on as mentioned in Mahabharta or Ramayana or Bhagwat Purana. It may be mentioned that various names were given to these crafts such as Sippa, Shilpa, Kalas etc, which have been mentioned as 64 Kalas out of which Nos. of industrial Kalas are around 28 only.

So far as the technology employing machinery and allied equipment is concerned, the first evidence in this regard is available in Ramayana only. An aeroplane called 'Pushpak Viman' was chartered to serve as convoy of Lord Rama which originally belonged to Ravana, is the example. Also the army which accompanied Bharta to meet Shri Rama in jungle to persuade him back to Ayodhya was all equipped with machines and other equipments for building bridges etc.

ARCHITECTURE :

Architecture in ancient India originated in the religious need of constructing Yajna-vedies/altars and halls for the performance of vedic sacrifice. The vedies were built in different forms, such as "Falcon" "Chariot" and many other shapes and designs necessitating architectural skill. A vedic fire altar is also traced in a hollow cave, hemispherical in shape, and with an opening like a chimney at the centre, discovered at Cannanore in Malabar. Next there is a mention of the walls and fortification of the old city of Rajagriha (Raigir) and remains of houses, built of rubble and rough eyclopean masonary, are the rare examples of such structures of durable material in that age. These ruins were of the time of Bimbisara (603-551 B.C.), the founder of Giribbaja hill-fort who changed the capital later to new Rajagriha. His architect and town planning expert is named as Mahagovinda.

Shore temple at Mahabalipuram

Fig. 6

ARCHITECTURE HAS TAKEN A FAST STRIDE IN SOUTH INDIAN TEMPLES

MEENAKSHI TEMPLE AT MADURAI

During the epic period, the city of Ayodhya presented the picture of highly developed state of architecture. Further the palace of king Yudhistra in the Mahabharta is described as lofty as the peaks of the Kailash mountain, most charming in appearance and provided with excellent furniture.

Advancement of Architecture during Maurya period: Chandra Gupta and Bindusara ruled for nearly half a century till about 273 B.C. A good idea of architectural development could be formed from the account of Megasthenes who lived in the Court of Chandra Gupta as an ambassador as under:

"The capital Pataliputra (modern Patna) at the confluence of the Ganges and the sone rivers was the greatest city in India. It was about a mile in length and a mile and a half in breadth. The wooden wall of the city, probably built of massive Saltrees, had 64 gates and was crowned with 510 towers. Surrounding the wall was a ditch, six hundred feet in breath, and thirty cubics in depth. The royal palace within city was one of the finest in the whole world, and its gilded pillars adorned with golden vines and silver birds extorted the admiration of the Greeks."

The period of Ashoka

The advent of Ashoka provided new dimension and direction to Indian art as well as architecture. Though, Maurya may be said to be a culminating point in the progress but no congnent evidence exists before the time of Ashoka.

The artistic and architectural achievements of Ashoka may be dassified under the following heads:

1. Stupas. 2. Pillars.

3. Caves. 4. Residential buildings.

Out of the above works of Ashoka, the stone pillars furnish the best specimen of sculpture and architecture. It is not possible to determine the total number of pillars erected by Ashoka's command, but the number may be set down between thirty and forty, if not more. Each of these columns consists mainly of two parts, the shaft and the capital. The shaft is monolithic i.e. made up of the piece of stone'.[8] As regards the palace, the Chinese pilgrim Fa-Hien writes.

Fig. 7

8. Mahabharta Sastragrahan Vidya vii, 23,29.

"The royal palace and halls in the midst of the city which exists now as of old, were all made by spirits which he employed and which piled up the stones, reared the walls and gates, and executed the elegant carving and inlaid sculpture work - in a way which no human hands of this world could accomplish".

TREATISE ON ARCHITECTURE:

As regards the authentic treatise on architecture 'Mansara' is the first exhaustive and authentic work on the science of architecture of about 7th century A.D. containing 42 chapters dealing with architecture. The treatise also furnishes an ideas about the training that was given to the architects and sculptures. It transpires that these twin professions had reached a stage of great perfection in those days.[9] According to Mansara, there has been 32 authorities on architecture and this science has come to the sages from Shiva, Brahma and Vishnu through Indra, Brihaspati, Narada and all other sages. The four faces of Brahma originated, the four heavenly architects viz Vishwakarma, Maya, Tvasti and Manu, and their four sons represent the guild of modern architects.[10]

---

9. Legge, Fa-Hien, p. 77.
10. P.K. Acharya, Indian Architechture As based on Mansara, Oxford, 1927.

MATHEMATICS

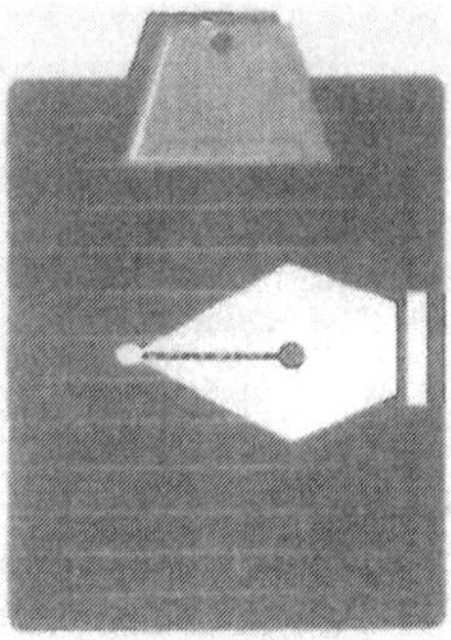

Fig. 8

The inception of mathematics of ancient India perhaps lies in the necessity of counting arisen in ancient man. The number of cattle or fruits like mangoes etc or other items in the beginning were perhaps counted with the help of small pebbles or fingers and different name must have been given to speak out the numbers. The system worked well when the number is very small.

In ancient India, during vedic period it was Medhatithi who has the singular credit to state even the high numerals in a systematic way. He extended the numerals to billions.

DEVELOPMENT OF PLACE VALUE NOTATION SYSTEM

Medhatithi provided a method to state numerals with multiples of 10 right up to billions and this resulted into development of place value system under which the symbols, the digit 1-9 and also 0 were deployed in such a way that the places of numerals indicated their value in multiple of 10. For example, in numeral 28 the place of 2, which is second from the right, means 20 but if the number is 281 then the place of 2 will be third from right and it will mean 200. This system emerged in 200 A.D and has tremendous importance in the development of mathematics. In fact it laid the foundation of mathematics.

Most of the historians of mathematics agree that the place-value in Indian number systems is something, which was developed entirely by the Indians. They have an interesting theory as to why the Indians might be pushed into such an idea. The reason, Joseph a mathematical historian believes, is due to the Indian fascination with large numbers. Freudenthal is another historian of mathematics who supports the theory that the idea came entirely from within Indians who have fascination with large numbers. We can take a look at the *Lalitavistara* which is an account of the life of Gautama Buddha. It is hard to date this work since it underwent continuous development over a long period but dating it to around the first or second century AD is reasonable. In *Lalitavistara* Gautama, when he is a young man, is examined on mathematics. He is asked to name all the numerical ranks beyond a koti, which are 10^7. He lists the powers of 10 up to 10^{53}. Taking this as a first level he then carries on to a second level and gets eventually to 10^{421}. Gautama's examiner says:-

You, not I, are the master mathematician.

It is stories such as this, and many similar ones, which convinces historians that the fascination of the Indians with large numbers must have driven them to invent a system in which such numbers are easily expressed, namely " place-valued notation."

The place value system use around 200 A.D. Aryabhatta and Varahamira the famous mathematicians and astronomer used their very system in fourth and fifth century A.D.

In Arabian countries this place value notation system came from India in 8th century A.D and the credit goes to Indian scholars who passed on this system to them. In Europe this system came in as late as in 10th century A.D.

DEVELOPMENT & WRITING OF NUMERALS

The necessity felt in writing the counted number of an item gave birth to numerals. The beginning might have been done by marking straight scratches on stone, earth or wall. There are evidences in Rig Veda that small numbers were written in symbol form as we read a scripture "give me a thousand cows from whose yores the number 8 is indicated". This speaks that some symbol was used for number 8. Similarly in Agni purana which was supposed to have been composed in 200 A.D, some symbols were used for 1,2 etc. By Earth, Moon or God denoting numeral 1. For numeral 2, pair of hands or eyes etc was denoted, but how the numeral 0,1,2,3,4,5,6,7,8,9, which we recognized today came in is a long history and Historians trace them all back to the Brahmi numerals came into being around the middle of the third century BC. Under which numbers 1,2,3 are represented by lines thereafter by symbols.

There were separate Brahmi symbols for 4, 5, 6, 7, 8, 9 but there were also symbols for 10, 100, 1000, ... as well as 20, 30, 40, ..., 90 and 200, 300, 400, ..., 900.

The Brahmi numerals have been found in inscriptions in caves and on coins in regions near Poona, Bombay, and Uttar Pradesh. Dating these numerals tells us that they were in use over quite a long time span up to the 4th century AD. Of course different inscriptions differ somewhat in the style of the symbols.

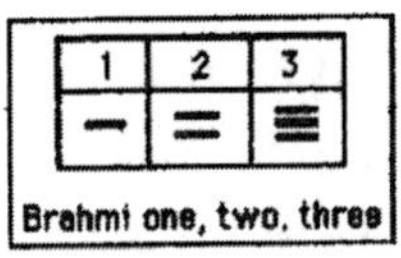

Brahmi one, two, three

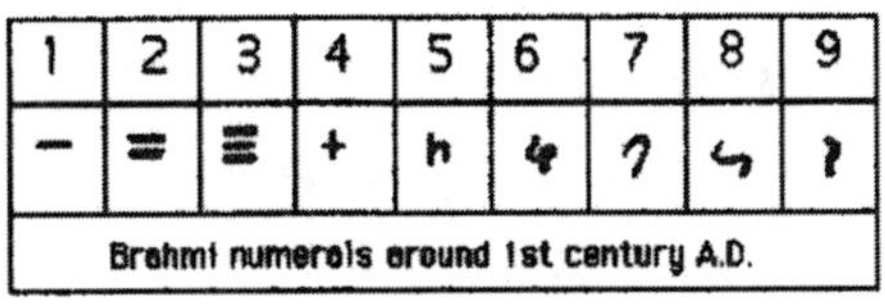

Brahmi numerals around 1st century A.D.

(Here is one style of the Brahmi numerals)

However, there are different theories concerning the origin of the Brahmi numerals. If we examine the route which led from the Brahmi numerals to our present symbols (and ignore the many other systems which evolved from the Brahmi numerals) let us come to the Gupta symbols. The Gupta period is that during which the Gupta dynasty ruled over the Magadha state in northeastern India, and this was from the early 4th century AD to the late 6th century AD. The Gupta numerals developed from the Brahmi numerals and were spread over large areas by the Gupta Empire as they conquered territory.

1	2	3	4	5	6	7	8	9	0
१	२	३	४	५	६	७	८	९	०

Nagari numerals around 11th century A.D.

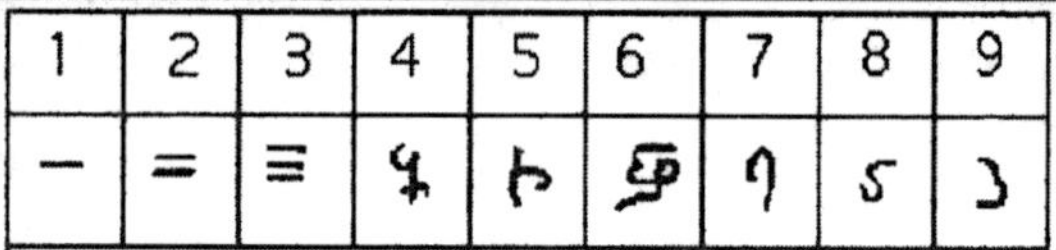

Gupta numerals around 4th century A.D.

The Gupta numerals evolved into the Nagari numerals, sometimes called the Devanagari numerals. This form evolved from the Gupta numerals beginning around the 7th century AD and continued to develop from the 11th century onward. The name literally means the "writing of the gods" and it was the considered the most beautiful of all the forms which evolved. For example Al-Biruni writes:-

"What we [the Arabs] use for numerals is a selection of the best and most regular figures in India".

These "most regular figures" which Al-Biruni refers to are the Nagari numerals, which had, by his time, been transmitted into the Arab world. The way in which the Indian numerals were spread to the rest of the world between the 7th to the 16th centuries is a long story. However, some of the historians claim that Indian numerals had reached Southern Europe by the end of the 5th century.

ASTRONOMY

The science of observing stars grew to have an idea regarding the day time and night time and also the appropriate time of sowing, harvesting as well as to prepare themselves for i.e, winter, summer and rainy season.

It was dawned upon the ancients that there are some bright stars in the sky, which do not change the position and that Moon at night and Sun during the day time move along a certain fixed heavenly path in the sky. It was also noticed that a group of movable stars could be used to know the position of Sun and Moon and the time of arising the Sun or setting the Sun or time of winter, summer or rains when the Sun has reached a particular group of stars, which were called Nakshatra or

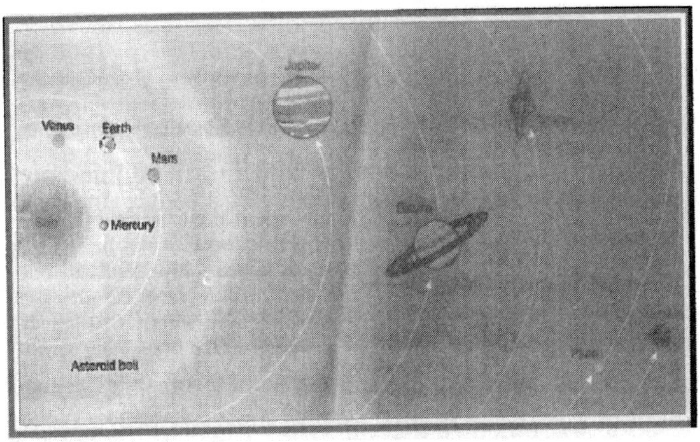

Fig. 9

constellations. Garga is the first one to enumerate these constellation followed by Lagadha who systematised all the available astronomical knowledge marking a significant development of astronomy in ancient India.

INDIAN ASTRONOMY ENRICHED BY GREEK CONTACTS :

The contacts with Greek started from the time of invasion of India in 327 BC by Alexander. Though the Greeks were driven out of India by Saka Kings before Ist Century BC, however the academic exchanges continued and these contacts enriched the astronomy further. Greek influence is clearly seen in various Indian Astronomical Siddhanatas such as Surya Siddhanata; Romaka Siddhanata and Poulisa Siddhanata etc.

It is worth mentioning that Vatasyan has given the several names of the ancient astronomers who contributed significantly to the development of Indian astronomy.

The list includes the names - Lomasa and Paulsa who appear basically Greek speaking clearly the assimilation of Greek knowledge of astronomy with Indian counterpart. In 5th century AD Aryabhatta provided a significant boost to the development of astronomy and he contradicted the orthodox views stating earth was a square sphere rotating on its axis and eclipses were not caused by Rahu but by the shadows of Moon and Earth. Varahamira and Brahma Gupta also contributed to the development of astronomy and expounded several siddhanatas in this regard though they disagreed that the Earth rotate on its axis. They also utilized the algebraic knowledge to solve various astronomy problems.

SIXTY FOUR KALAS

In many Buddhist and Jain works there is mention of various arts and vocations which were called as 'kalas' and the traditional number has been mentioned as sixty four though some works mention more than 64 kalas. The details of traditional 64 kalas have been given in many works such as Kadambini, Kamsutra by 'Vatsayana etc. The disciplines of crafts and technology have been sorted out from the list of 64 kalas as under:

1. Metallurgy
2. Mine Technology
3. Military science
4. Science of archery
5. Cooking technology
6. Leather technology
7. Textile design technology
8. Textile technology
9. Machine fabrication technology
10. Earth work technology
11. Machine construction technology
12. Dairy technology
13. Ship building technology

14. Gold technology
15. Weapon manufacturing technology

The commonly mentioned 64 kalas complied on the basis of knitisara are as under:

1. Dancing
2. Skill of playing on many instruments together in a concert.
3. Skill in decorating men and women with dress and ornaments
4. Art of producing various forms of figures out of stone, wood, and other materials, the art of the sculpture.
5. The art of making beds and garlands with flowers.
6. The art of entertaining by gambling and other past times.
7. Anekasanasandhanairratexjnanam.
8. The skill of preparing flower-juice and other intoxicating liquors.
9. Skill of extracting burned arrows, spears etc. and of incision of open wounds and blood vessels.
10. Skill of cooking various dishes with the various rases combined in different proportions.
11. Grafting and planting and culture of plants.
12. Melting and reducing to ashes stones, minerals and the like.
13. Skill of the preparation of things from the juice of sugar-cane.
14. Minerals and herbs.

15. Producing new compounds of minerals.
16. Skill of combining and isolating minerals.
17. Extracting the kshararase out of minerals.

Fig. 10

18. The art of adjusting the bow with the foot, fitting the arrow and then shooting it.
19. The art of wrestling in different ways, utilising grips and falls of diverse kinds.
20. Skill of hurling weapons and missiles at observed marks.
21. The knowledge of forming an army into Vyuhas in accordance with the direction conveyed by instrumental music.
22. Taking part in battle on elephant, horse, or chariot.
23. Propitiating details by worship in different postures and by different mudras of dispositions of fingers.
24. The science of charioteering.
26. The art of producing vessels and the like out of such materials as clay, wood, stone or metals.

Fig. 11

25. The art of training elephants and horses in movements.
27. Painting of pictures.
28. The art of excavating tanks and wells and levelling the ground.
29. Construction of machines like the water-wheel and of musical instruments, apparatus, engineszt etc. as explained by Williams and use of machines.
30. The art of painting with colours mixed in different proportions or quantities, large, moderate and the like.
31. Working with water fire and air in two ways by utilizing them or by controlling them.
32. The science and art of constructing ships, chariots and other vehicles for locomotion.
33. The art of making yarns, ropes etc.

34. Weaving of cloth out of a variety of yarns.
35. The science of testing precious stones and of the processes of cutting and boring them and similar processes.
36. The art of examining the properties of gold and testing its genuineness.
37. The science and art of manufacturing artificial gold and imitation precious stones.
38. The art of enamelling, polishing, varnishing etc.
39. Manufacture of ornaments from materials like gold.
40. The science and art of training leather.
41. The science of separating the hide and the various limbs from the bodies of animals.
42. Knowledge of the processes of milking and of making ghee from milk as its ultimate product.
43. Skill of sewing bodices.
44. Skill of swimming in water with hands.
45. Skill of cleansing houses and household utensils land furniture.
46. Skill of shaving.
47. Skill of extracting the essence out of sesame, meats and fat.
48. The skill of ploughing, sowing etc.
49. Skill of climbing tree and the like
50. The art of serving another to his heart's content.
51. The skill of making vessels out of bamboo, reeds etc.

52. The science of manufacturing vessels, lamps other articles out of glass.
53. The science of irrigation by which water is distributed and collected.
54. Manufacturing weapons out of metals.
55. Manufacturing of saddles etc. to be used for riding elephants, horses, bricks and camels.
56. The art of bringing up, handling and playing with children.
57. The art of handling offernders by suitable rebukers.
58. The art of preparing taimbula i.e. betel-nuts, areca, nuts, slaked lime etc.
59. Proficiency in writing the alphabets of various countries.
60. Power of comprehension of these kalas.
61. Quickness of work.
62. Imparting instruction in the kalas.
63. Slow or gradual work.

3

Ancient Scientists and Engineers

ANCIENT SCIENTISTS AND ENGINEERS

India the *Bharatvarsha* named after the king Bharta[1] has given birth to great Rishies , Saints sages, scientists and engineers who were the great personalities of their period and tried to give logical answer to various problems connected with the life and universe around us. These saints and scientists of ancient India devoted themselves in the pursuit of scientific

A view of the Lomasrishi Cave, Barabar Hills

1. Bharta - A great king of Ancient India on whose name this country is called Bharat Varsh. Earlier India was called Ajnabha.

knowledge, leaving and renunciating the world and set up their hermitage at a secluded place. What is more remarkable, is the fact that neither money nor fame nor any material gain has been the motive of these saints and rishies of ancient India. What they wrote, they wrote for self fulfilment as inner urge 'Savanta Sukhay' The bhoj patra in absence of paper in those days was used as writing material, and in many cases only one copy of original manuscript was prepared by them which during the course of time was not preserved well and either some leaves got detatched or the manuscript itself became untraceable after the death of the greatman.

No precise account is available regarding the place of birth, death and anticedents of family etc. of many of our ancient scientists. The manuscripts which they wrote working hard also underwent alteration, deletion and recenssion and what is available today, is not in the original form in which these were composed-Carka Samhita, Susurta Sanihita and many other such works are the examples. This has resulted into a situation that we only know very little about our great saints and scientists. It is only through the hard work recently done by certain European historians that we are able to gather some knowledge about our ancient genious.

Versatility of Ancient Scientists

The modern age is of specialty, be it science, medicine, or engineering. An eye specialist is only concerned with the problem pertaining to opthalmology. Similarly, a civil engineer

will devote himself only to the construction and structural aspect of buildings, roads, canals etc. and will not bother about the other disciplines of engineering i.e. electronics, mechanical etc. An atomic scientist will also limit himself to the atomic field. In ancient India, however, the scientists and engineers were having versatile personality and knowledge. Bhardavaja who was a vedic rishi and figures in Rigveda having contributed to the hymns of Rigveda was not only a Rishi alone. As a result of research several manuscripts have been discovered and attributed to Rishi Bhardavaja on aeronautic science, hydraulics and even designing of aeroplanes. Similarly. Viswamitra[2] who also figures as a Vedic rishi designed a mechanical device and appratus to produce fire through attrition. Varahmiha was not only a astronomer but demonstrated his vast knowledge in agriculture and other fields. Susurata who is considered as the father of surgery was a agriculturist and a Botanist also. This shows the multifarious personality and knowledge of our scientists.

---

2. अस्तीदमधितमन्थनमस्ति प्रजननं कृतम्।
एतां विश्पन्तीमा भराग्निं मन्थाम पूर्वथा।। (1)
अरण्योर्निहितो जातवेदा गर्भ इव सुधितो गर्भिणीषु।
दिवेदिव ईडयो जागृवद्भिर्हविष्मद्भिर्मनुष्योभिरग्निः।। (2)
उत्तानायामव भरा चिकित्वान्त्सद्यः प्रवीता वृषणां जजान।
अरुषस्तूपो रुशदस्य पाज इठायास्पुत्रो वयुनेऽजनिष्ट।।(3)

–Rv. III.29.12

Scientists through various periods of ancient India

Vedic Period

The vedic period is considered one of the most ancient periods in Indian History. It was the age of tapas, yogas and maditation. The great rishies devoted themselves in practicing austerities seeking truth and self realization. This period has seen many a rishies and rishikas. The perusal of Rigveda and other vedas show that the following rishies are associated with the Rigveda hymns.

Attri (son of Bhumi) Kasyapa (son of Marica) Gotama (belonging to Rahugana) Jamadagni (son of Bhrgu) Bhardavaja (belonging to the school of Brhaspati) Vasistha (belonging to Mitravaruna) and Visvamitra (the son or disciple of Cathin). The same Seven Seers are associated with other verses, and many of them have contributed to the knowledge of sciences of very high order. Among others Garga, Lagdha and Medhalithi are the illusterious names in the field of astronomy and mathematics.

Later Vedic Period

The Rigveda discusses two clear streams of religious thoughts. The original stream of pure thought was that enuciated by rishies -the direct seers of truth and is marked by meditation, contemplation and tapas. However, the second stream comprises of sacrifical rituals and priesthood. By the end of

Vedic period the second stream dominated and religion was bogged down by ceremonial sacrifices with its details more and more elaborated. The auspicious time and day for performing fire-sacrificing i.e. Yajna assumed significance and dominance. The later vedic period from 800 to 300 B.C. is marked with galaxy of various preceptors and scientists in various specialities including astronomy as well as the medical science and surgery. We have Bhardavaja[3], Attrey and Charka in Ayurvedic medicines. Patanjali in Yoga doctrine and Susurata in surgery, then Baudhyana the great geometror, similarly Kanda the ancient atomic philosopher scientist are the shining stars of this age.

Mauryas, Nandas and Gupta period

The period of Maurya including the Ashoka the great and Gupta age is considered to be a golden one where in all around development in science, art and literature took place. Varahmihra, Nagarjuna and Arya Bhatta are the famous names which added glory to the period of ancient India. In post Harsha period we have signs of decadence and very few personalities in ancient science and technology made their mark except Bhaskara in South India and some alchemists etc. The reasons for the declination have already been discussed in the earlier chapter.

---

3. गान्धर्व नारदो वेदं भरद्वाजो धनुर्ग्रहम्।
देवर्षि चरितं गार्ग्यः कृष्णात्रेयश्चिकित्सतम्।।

– Mahabharata Sani Chapter 210

Prejudiced attitude of European historians

A prejudiced approach has been made, unfortunately by various European historians towards the glorious past of India. They perhaps can not forget that they belong to the imperial race which held India in political subjection for a century. While India is grateful to European scholars to have rendered their valuable services of collecting material for ancient Indian history and civilization, they some time do not cast aside the assumption of racial superiority.

Lord Macauley -an English Educationist and who has been the Chief of Public Instructions in British India and has been responsible for introduction of English in India minced no words for betraying his prejudiced approach as will be seen from the following :

i) "A single shelf of a good European literature was worth the whole native literature of India and Arabia".

ii) About teaching through the media of Sanskrit and Arabic he stated "*we* are to teach false history, false astronomy, false medicine because we find them in the company of a false religion".

Discovery of the glorified past of India

Some of the early oriental as well as the European scholars did render a valuable service for India to have brought home the glorified past and greatness of ancient India, worth mentioning names are William Jones, Max Mullar, Wilson etc.

Mr. H. Kern brought out an edition of the 'Aryabhattiya' and Whitney and Burgess translated the Suryasiddhanta in 1860. Through these texts, the Indian Astronomy was rediscovered for the modern western scholars. Scholars like Sir William Jones and H.T. Colebrooke brought the literary treasures of India to the notice of the English speaking world. As early as 1823, Prof. H.H. Wilson published his Essay on the 'Medical and Surgical Science of the Hindus', and this was followed by 'Essay on the Antiquity of Hindu Medicine' by J.R Royle in 1837 and also; T.A. Wise's 'A Commentary on the Hindu System of Medicine in 1845' .

4

Bhardwaja

- A Great Vedic Rishi
- Pioneer of Ayurvedic Medicine
- A Scientist – An Engineer

4

BHARDWAJA

• A Great Vedic Rishi

• Pioneer of Ayurvedic Medicine

• A Scientist – An Engineer

Bhardwaja has an important place in Vedic chronology. He has been mentioned as a vedic Rishi and is one of the six representative Rishies whose works were utilised to constitute the six different Mandals i.e. 2 to 6 of the Rig Veda and show considerable literary skill originality and insight into various religious deeds.

The seven commonly known Vedic Rishies are regarded as under :

No. 1. – Images in stone of seven Vedic Rishis.
(1) Vasishtha (2) Visvamitra
(3) Vamadeva (4) Bharadvaja
(5) Atri (6) Kanva (7) Gritsamada

BHARDWAJA AS FATHER OF INDIAN MEDICINE

Ayurveda the science of medicine also owes its inception to great sage Bhardwaja and his line of descent is from Angires. There are various medicinal receipes attributed to him. As per account available in Caraka Sanhita, Bhardwaja presided the first symposium on medicinal plants relating to various diseases. This symposium was held in regions of Himalyas 7th century B.C., the details of which quoted from Carka-Sanhita are as under :[1]

(1) When diseases arose like so many impediments to the austerity, fasting, study, continence and vows of men in general, the great sages, the doers of good, imbibed with compassion for creatures foremost, met togather on the sacred slopes of the Himalayas.

(2) Bharadvaja, the mighty ascetic, in search of the science of longevity approached Indra, having deemed him, the lord of the immortals, worthy of suit.

---

1. विघ्नभूता यदा रोगाः प्रादुर्भूताः शरीरिणाम्।
तपोपवासाध्ययन-ब्रह्मचर्यव्रतायुषाम्॥
तदा भूतेष्वनुक्रोशं पुरस्कृत्य महर्षयः।
समेताः पुण्यकर्माणः पार्श्वे हिमवतः शुभे॥

– Caraka. Sn. I. 6-7

तेनायुरमितं लेभे भरद्वाजः सुखान्वितम्।
ऋषिभ्योऽनधिकं तञ्च शशंसानवशेषयन्॥
ऋषयश्च भरद्वाजाज्जगृहुस्तं प्रजाहितम्।
दीर्घमायुश्चिकीर्षन्तो वेदं वर्धनमायुषः॥ **– Caraka. Sn. I. 26-27**

(3) Daksa Prajapati the progenitor, first obtained the Science of Life in its entirety as promulgated by Brahma the Great one, i.e., the Creator and from Him, in turn, the Asvina Twins obtained it. From the Asvina Twins the god Sakra (Indra) acquired it. Therefore Bharadvaja bidden by the sages approached Sakra.

(4) He taught the science of causes, symptoms and medication, the supreme refuge of both-the healthy and the ailing, the tripartite science, eternal and holy, which the Great Father Brahma, knew.

(5) He, the sage of great understanding, soon learned correctly, by single-minded devotion, the whole Science of Life, tri-based and extending without end.

(6) Bharadvaja thereby acquired unmeasured life endowed with happiness, and in his turn, taught the science to the sages, without either adding or withholding any part.

(7) And the sages, desiring longevity, received from Bharadvaja that science, beneficial to humanity and promotive of life.

BHARDWAJA AS PRECEPTOR

Bhardwaja figures as a preceptor or Rishi in Ramayana with his hermitage at Prayaga and as per description given in Ramayna Lord Rama accompanied with Laxman and Sita had a brief halt at his hermitage and got religious discourse from him. The hermitage of Bhardwaja has also been shown in Bharat scripture which are supposed to be of 2nd century B.C.

BIGGEST ASHRAMA OF THE TIME

The hermitage of Bhardwaja at Prayaga as per account available in Ramayana was the biggest ashrama of the time which accommodated Bharata and his entourage including the ladies of the Palace. The Ashrama was equipped with "White Chatuh salas", stalls which accommodated the royal elephants and horses; harmyas or mansions; parasadas or palaces, and their toranas or gateways; royal guest-house fitted with several toranas, and furnished with beds, seats and vehicles, coverlets and carpters, stores of food. The Ashrama also entertained its royal guests with the performance of musicians and dancing girls. All this lavish hospitality was of the area provided for the occasion, showing the resources which Rishi Bhardwaja could command in the locality by his personality.

Bhardwaja as a scientist Engineer. An entirely new light has been thrown on the versatality of Bhardwaja following the discovery of three menuscripts :

1. Vaimanik Prakarnam (Aeronautical science)
2. Kritka Vajra Nirnay (Preparation of artificial diamonds)
3. *Jal Tatva Parakarnam (Hydrology)*

These manuscripts deal with scientific concepts and seem to be founded on a self contained and in the scientific system of frame work largely unknown to the present system of modern science. In fact they are based on scientific concepts unique to ancient India (See Hindustan Times dated 25-2-91). The discovery shows that Bhardwaja was a scientist or engineer or both.

BIRTH AND AGE OF BHARDWAJA

As per mythical story mentioned in Yayu Purana and Mahabharta, Bhardwaja was the son of Nany by Brhaspati. While as transpires from Carak-Sanhita and other scriptures his descent is from the Atharvan and Angries who are pioneer to propagate fire. Infact quite a several Bhardwajas have been referred to in the vedic literature and Epic Bhardwaja lived a large life of three generation of man. But there is a gap of several centuries between vedic, Epic and age of Puranas. What is safe is to suggest that instead of being single individual Bhardwaja was an institution? There is immense contribution of Bhardwaja in literary, medical and ancient scriptures.

BHARDWAJA

Birth and Age

Son of Nany by Brhaspati

(Ref. Vayupurana & Mahabharata)

Important Works

(As per recent discovery)

- *Vaimanik prakarnam(Aeronautical sciences)*
- *Kritka vajra nirnay(preparation of artificial diamonds)*
- *Jal tatva parakarnam(hydrology)*

Achievements

- *A great vedic Rishi*
- *Regarded as pioneer of Ayurvedic Medicine*
- *An expounder of New scientific concepts unknown to modern science.*

5

Dhanvantari
A God Physician

5

DHANVANTARI A GOD PHYSICIAN

Susruta in his monumental work, *Susruta Samhita,* ac knowledge the greatest of all Ayurvedic physicians on the Earth, Lord Dhanvantari, for the knowledge of *Salya-tantra* (the science of surgery) and other sacred doctrines of Ayurveda.

BIRTH MYTH AND LEGEND

Birth of Dhanvantari is related to many myths and legends. According to one popular story he emerged from the Milky Ocean *(Kshira Sagara)* during its churning by the Gods and Demons for obtaining *amrita* (the elixir of immortality). Vie is regarded as an incarnation of Lord Vishnu, the preserver of the Universe and a disciple of Lord Siva, the conqueror of Yama (the king of Death). Thus he embraces the quality of *amrii 'a* which is the panacea for all diseases. According to another story Dhanvantari was born to a young maiden named Virbhadr by the divine blessings of sage Galvana. Dhanvantari is said to have married the three daughters of Asvini Kumara and became the father of fourteen sons. He is said to have taught surgery to Susruta and many other students.

FIGHT FOR SUPREMACY

One story illustrates a legendary fight between Dhanvantari and the Goddess of Serpents. named Manasa which culminated in the humiliation of the great physician. It indicates the limitations of medicinal power in certain circumstances. It also throws light on Ayurveda's close proximity with prayers, meditations and other devotional practices in ancient India. Even today the great physicians of the world admit the blessings of some external power that can only save the patient in certain circumstances.

The Vedas do not give any information regarding Dhanvantari. He was the god of Ayurveda and is still held in high esteem. The 'Dhanvantari Award' is presented to an Avurvedic physician who attains the highest perfection in modern times and is conferred with the title of "Dhanvantari".

DHANWANTRI

AT A GLANCE

Age And Birth

Full of many myths & legends.

Contribution

- *Believed to have taught surgery to Susurta and many other students.*
- *Regarded as an incarnation of lord Vishnu.*

6

Vishwamitra

- A Vedic Rishi
- The first founder of Engineering

6

VISHWAMITRA

- **A Vedic Rishi**
- **The First Founder of Engineering**

Imagine the life without fire. No bread to eat, no cooked vegetables, no boiled rice, milk is also cool and raw, no cream is formed, neither any butter nor cheese. Also, in winter weather one would not have warm water to bath. Almost all the eatables and dishes, necessiate the use of fire. Such was the situation of ancient people of any civilization and also of the most ancient period of India. Though, it was Atharvan who discovered the fire for the first time according to vedic texts and various hymns there in. However, Vishwamitra appears to be first Rishi who provided the first device to generate fire and in modern sense could be termed as founder of engineering.

Vishwamitra is also regarded as a vedic Rishi and an exclusive one Mandal of Rig Veda is his greatest contribution and all the hymns of Rig Veda in the mandal owe their authorship to Vishwamitra. Not only Rigveda, Vishvamitra is the Rishi of a number of verses of the Atharvaveda also :

III, 17; V. 15-16, VI. 44,141-142, XX. 1, 1; 6; 7, 4; 8, 3, 11; 13, 4; 19; 20; 1-4; 23-24; 57, 4-7; 86; 102.

We also find Vishwamitra in the age of Ramayana when he approaches king Dashratha to seek the help of his divine sons Sri Ram and Laxman to protect his Yajnas. Vishwamitra also figures in Mahabharta where there is a reference containing the names of his several sons.

In view of the above, there may be two possibilities, one is that Vishwamitra was not an individual but an institution mentioned during the Vedic period, Ramayana period as well as Mahabharata period. The other explanation results from the belief that age of a true rishi transcends the barrier of a normal span of longevity and goes to several hundred years and the epic period if considered to follow immediately after vedic period, the Rishi Vishwamitra might have lived till Mahabharata period in that case.

VISHWAMITRA AS FOUNDER OF ENGINEERING:

Vishwamitra is the first founder of Engineering of ancient India. The development of human culture of any race is linked with the harnessing of fire which though appears a very common phenomnon now-a-days. Rekindling of fire if it dies out, has been a problem of ancient civilisations as the methods employed for producing the fire were very tiresome.

Vishwamitra appears to be the first who used the mechanical means for harnessing the fire by devising a apparatus of attrition. This is evinced from the hymns of Rigveda. III 29.1-12[1]

1. This the appratus of artrition is ready, the generation (of the flame) is ready, rake up this (stick), the protectress

of manking and let us churn the fire as has been done of old.

2. Jatavedas has been deposited in the two sticks as the embryo is deposited in pregnant woman. Agni is to be adored day by day by vigilant men laden with oblations.

3. Let the intelligent priest place the lower of the sticks with the face upwards, the upper (with the surface downwards so that quickly impregted it may generate the showere (of benefits) Agni : than the bright blazing son of Ila, whose light dissipates the darkness is born of the wood of attriction.

4. Agni, who art Jatavedas, we place thy upon the earth in the center, in the place of Ila, for the purpose of receiving the oblation.

5. Conductors of the rite, produce by attrition, the farseeing, single-minded, intelligent, immortal, radiant-limbed Agni : generate him, leaders (of the solemnity), in the first place the chief standard of the sacrifice, who is the source of felicity.

---

1. इलायास्त्वा पदे वयं नाभा पृथिव्या अधि।
जातवेदो नि धीमह्यग्ने हव्याय वोलहवे॥ (4)
मन्थता नरः कविमद्वयन्तं प्रचेतसममृतं सुप्रतीकम्।
यज्ञस्य केतुं प्रथमं पुरस्तागिन नरो जनयता सुशेवम्॥(5)
यदी मन्थन्ति बाहुभिर्वि रोचतेऽश्वो न वाज्यरुषो वनेष्वा।
चित्रो न यामत्रश्विनोरनिवृतः परि वृणाक्त्यश्मनस्तृरणा दहन्॥(6)

Rig Veda 29.4-6

6. When they rub (the sticks) with their arms, the radiant Agni bursts forth from the wood like a fleet courser and like the many-coloured car of the Asvins unresisted in its course, Agni spreads wide around consuming stones and trees.

7. As soon as born Agni shines intelligent, swift-moving, skilled in rites, praised by the wise, and liberal in gifts, (and it is he) whom the gods have held as the bearer of oblations at the scrifices, adorable and all knowing.

The hymn is associated with Vishvamitra son of Gathin who devised the mechanical method of producing fire by friction, Construction of the apparatus of attrition, consisting of the stick, the string and the like, placed upon the two pieces of wood to assist in their attrition, a tuft to dry grass used to catch and communicate the flame.

The above hymns are the clear evidence that Vishwamitra was having the necessary engineering skill by virtue of which he was able to devise the apparatus of attrition and in this way he could be rightly called as the first founder of engineering in ancient India.

7

Garga
The Pioneer of Astrology

7

GARGA - THE PIONEER OF ASTROLOGY

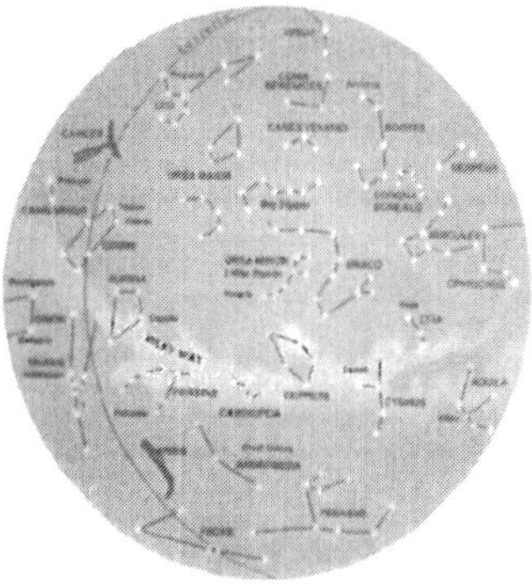

Imagine the life of early times when there was no watch, no clock to give time or to furnish an idea about morning, forenoon, afternoon and evening, no one could say whether it is midnight or so.

The ancients found the way to meet the situation with the help of constellations which are a group of shining stars in the heavenly path-ecliptic considered immovable and are called Nakshatras. The position of sun and moon with respect to these constellations was used to furnish the idea about the season i.e. summer, winter, rainy and the position of day and night.

Garga was the first astronomer to have enumerated these constellations and the number was given as 28, which matches with many references in AthravVeda. Infact in the RigVeda also there is a mention of these constellations. However, the comprehensive details were given by Garga. He even correctly furnished the position of stars at the time of birth of LORD KRISHNA and as per Bhagvad Purana and Mahabharata he was "KUL PUROHIT" of Lord Krishna to have performed all the rituals from the birth to marriage ceremony of Shri Krishna.

AGE AND BIRTH OF GARGA

Nothing is precisely known about the birth and age of the great astronomer. The reference of his name available in Athrava Veda wherein several hymns are attributed to him suggest that he belonged to the Vedic period. However as per Mahabharata & Bhagvad Purana wherein his name figures prominently in several places he should be alive during that period also. The dichotomy lies in the fact that there is a gap of several centuries between the period of Athrava Veda and Mahabharta. This shows that Garga was not an individual but an institution standing for Astronomy and Astrology. Again as per ancient text Garga got the divine knowledge of stars from Shesha, the divine serpent whom he propiated and pleased through his rigorous tapas.

GARGA SANHITA

Garga Sanhita is a compendium about the star constellations and is based upon the views of Garga. However the Sanhita is believed to have been composed in third century B.C. as it contains the reference of Greek invasion of India and the Greeks have been termed as MALCHHAS. This shows that Sanhita composed later on is the revised version of an early work, the original of which has been lost as happened to many a scripts of other scientists of India. The constellations are still considered very important in Indian Astrology to predict the luck, success and status of a person.

GARGA

Age And Birth

Belongs to Vedic Period (Athar Veda)

Important Works

- *Garg Sanhita-A compendium about the star constellations (composed later on).*
- *First astronomer to have enumerated constellations.*

8

Medhatithi

First to Extend Numerals to Billions

8

MEDHATITHI - FIRST TO EXTEND NUMERALS TO BILLIONS

"The ingenious method of expressing every possible number using a set of ten symbols (each symbol having a place value and an absolute value) emerged in India. The idea seems so simple now a days that its significance and profound importance is no longer appreciated. Its simplicity lies in the way it facilitated calculation and placed arithmetic foremost amongst useful inventions. The importance of this invention is more readily appreciated when one considers that it was beyond the two greatest men of Antiquity archimedes and Apolloniusi"

(Laplace in the article over view of Indian Mathematics)

The comments of Laplace the famous Historian of math ematics note are worthy as well as important one and India can rightly raise its head high so far as development of Mathematics in ancient times is concerned. The place value system emerged in India is based upon the principles laid down by Medhatithi during Vedic times.

Counting the small number of items i.e. one, two, three, four could be done by pebbles or fingers but when the number is large, how to speak, was a problem, which has been tackled in different ways in different civilizations.

In ancient India during Vedic period it was Medhatithi who has the singular credit to state even the high numerals in a systematic way. He extended the numerals to billions.

Medhatitlit belonged to Kanwa family, which has the distinction of having given berth to many Rig Vedic seers. The name of Medhatithi is associated to a large number of Rig Vedic hymns (as many as 313 verses) and also in Atharveda and Yajurveda. The multiples of 10 enumerated in Yajurveda is associated with the name of Medhatithi which is one of the contribution of India.

A verse associated with his name in Yajurveda lists the name of the numerals as follows.

"O Agni, may these bricks be mine on milch-kine;

Eka (one) and Dasa (ten), a Sata (hundred), Sahasra (thousand); ten thousands;

An Ayuta (a myriad); a ten Ayutas, a Niyuta (a hundred thousand); a ten Niyutas, a prayutta (one million); ten Prayutas,

---

3. इमा मे ऽअग्न ऽ इष्टका धेनवः सन्त्वेका व दश च शतं च सहस्रं च सहस्रं चायुतं चायुतं च नियुतं व प्रयुतं चाबुदं न्यर्वुद च तमुद्रक्ष्व मध्यं चान्तक्ष्व परार्धश्चैता में ऽ अग्न ऽ इष्टका धेनवः सन्तवमुत्रामुष्मिं ल्लोके।

— Yv. XVII.2

an Arbuda (ten millions); ten Arbudas, a Nyarbuda (one hundred millions); ten Nyarbudas, a Samudra (one thousand millions); ten Samudras, a Madhya (a ten thousand millions); ten Madhyas, an Anta (a hundred thousand millions); ten Antas, a Parardha (a million million or a billion). May theses bricks be mine own milche-Kine in yonder world and in this world.

Thus a Parardha is 10^{12}

The list of numerals is reproduced in the Taittiriya Samhita (IV.4.1 1).

DEVELOPMENT OF PLACE VALUE NOTATION SYSTEM

Medhatithi provided a method to state numerals with multiples of 10 right up to billions and this resulted into development of place value system under which the symbols, the digit 1-9 and also 0 were deployed in such a way that the places of numerals indicated their value in multiple of 10. For example, in numeral 28 the place of 2 which is second from the right, means 20 but if the number is 281 then the place of 2 will be third from right and it will mean 200. This system emerged in 200 A.D and has tremendous importance in the development of mathematics In fact, it laid the foundation of mathematics.

Most of historians of mathematics agree that the place-value in Indian number systems is something which was developed entirely by the Indians. They have an interesting theory as to why the Indians might be pushed into such an idea. The reason, Joseph a mathematical historian believes, is due to the Indian fascination with large numbers. Freudenthal is another historian of mathematics who supports the theory that the idea came entirely from within Indians who have fascination with large numbers, we can take a look at the *Lalitavistara* which is an account of the life of Gautama Buddha. It is hard to date this work since it underwent continuous development over a long period but dating it to around the first or second century AD is reasonable. In *Lalitavistara* Gautama, when he is a young man, is examined on mathematics. He is asked to name all the numerical ranks beyond a koti, which are 10^7. He lists the powers of 10 up to 10^{53}. Taking this as a first level he then carries on to a second level and gets eventually to 10^{421}. Gautama's examiner says:

You, not I, are the master mathematician.

It is stories such as this, and many similar ones, which convinces historians that the fascination of the Indians with large numbers must have driven them to invent a system in which such numbers are easily expressed, namely "place-valued".

> The place value system came in use around 200 A.D. Aryabhatta and Varahamira the famous mathematicians and astronomers used their very system in fourth and 15th century A.D.
>
> In Arabian countries this place value notation system came from India in 8th century A.D and the credit goes to Indian scholars who passed on this system to them. In Europe this system came in as late as in 10th century A.D.

MEDHATITHI

AT A GLANCE

Age And Birth

Belongs to Rig Vedic Period

Contribution

- *Provided a method to state numerals with multiples of 10 right up to billions.*
- *Laid the foundation of place value system*

9

Lagdha

A Great Astronomer

9

LAGDHA - A GREAT ASTRONOMER

Ancient Indian astronomy is indebted to Lagadha, as it was he who systemised the available astronomical knowledge in the form of treatise scattered in various ancient scriptures and made his significant contribution to enrich the science of stars. Rig-Veda and Athrav Veda contain hymns indicating that the ancients were known to the constellations and Garga has enumerated them as 28. However there was no regular text or compendium systemising the astronomical knowledge.

''NAKSHATRAS" in olden (ancient) times were used for calculating the auspicious time of performing religious rites and astronomy in ancient times was used to determine the appropriate time for various religious rites, performing Yajnas and other auspicious occasions. Even King Ashoka took the help of astronomy to calculate the time of launching Buddhist pilgrimage and to calculate its duration.

TIME AND AGE OF LAGDHA

The period in which Lagadha lived is around 900 B.C. and his famous work, "JYOTISHA VEDANGA" was also composed during this period probably in Kashmir Valley.

Lagadha's astronomy "JYOTISHA VEDANGA" contains the principle and system of astronomy expounded by Lagadha which is available in two versions, "Rig Veda Jyotisha" and "Yajur Veda Jyotisha" and both are more or less the same. As regards the contents and principles, following are the salient features of Lagadha's astronomy : -

1. A Yuga consists of a cycle of 5 years and Yuga began when the Sun and Moon arrive together at the "Dhanishta" constellation.
2. A year would have 366 days and accordingly the period of Yuga is of 18030 days.
3. Each month consists of 30 days each and ordinarily there were 12 months in a year. Since this works out 1800 days so a gap of 30 days was plugged up to interpolate 1 extra month of 30 days.
4. According to Lagadha there were 6 seasons in a year, each of 2 months.
5. A day consists of 30 Muhurataas and the day was started from Sunrise and ends at the next Sunrise.
6. There were 2 kinds of months mentioned - Lunar month and Civil month. Lunar month was the period between two New Moons and had 29+32/62 days; it means 30/62 part of the day shorter than Civil Month i.e. General

month. A Lunar day was called as "Thithi" and was less than Civil day by 1/62 part of a day.

7. Methods have been given for calculating the auspicious time for performance of religious sacrifices.

Jyotisha Vedanga was considered an important work and even the Jain religion in later times incorporated the basic principles of Jyotisha Vedanga.

LAGDHA

AT A GLANCE

Age & Birth

Around 900 B.C probably in Kashmir valley

Important Works

- *Jyotisha vadanga in two versions (Rigveda jyotisha, Yajurveda jyotisha)*

Achievements

- *The first to have a regular text or compendium on astronomy.*

10

Baudhayana
The First Great Geometer

10

BAUDHAYANA THE FIRST GREAT GEOMETER

Baudhayana (8th century B.C.) is considered to be the great geometer of ancient India. The science of geometry in ancient India developed with the yajnas or fire sacrifice which necessiated the construction of altars in Vedic civilization. In fact the whole culture and civilization of this land developed in ancient times owe their origin to yajnas. Altars were constructed to perform many kinds of Vedic sacrifices which were of two classes: (i) Nitya and (ii) Kamya. The Kamya sacrifices were performed with special motives and as per strict injunction laid-down. Such sacrifice must be performed in a altar of prescribed shape or size. It was the general belief of Aryans that even a slight irregularity in shape was enough to nullify the object of the whole ritual, therefore, necessiating the extra care in regard to the shape and size of the altar.

We have Sulbas or Sulba Sutras which are the works of several preceptors and are the manuals of construction of altaras. Out of all the Sulbas or Sulba Sutras, Baudhayana is the latest and biggest, and was composed by Baudhayana between 500-300 B.C. It is divided into 3 chapters. The first chapter contains 116 Sutras (aphorisms) of which the opening two are merely introductory; Sutras 3-21 define the various measures ordinarily employed in the Sulbas; Sutras 22-62 give the more important of the geometrical propositions necessary for the construction of the sacrificial altars; and Sutras 63-113 deal briefly with the relative positions and spatial magnitudes of the various Vedis (or altars).

The second chapter of the Baudhayana Sulba Sutra consists of 83 Sutras of which the major portion, Sutras 1-61 are devoted to the description of the special relations in the different constructions of the Agnis (or the large Fire altars made of bricks) in general, and the remaining portion, Sutras 62-83, elaborates the construction of the two simplest Agnis (The Garhapatyaciti or the House-holders, Fire-altar and Chandas-citi or the verse-altar, i.e., the Agni made, as it were ,or mantras instead of bricks). The third chapter contains altogether 323 Sutras and described the construction of as may as 17 different kinds of Kamya Agnis (or the altars for the sacrifices performed with a view to attain definite objects) of rather complex nature. In some cases, the descriptions by Baudhayana are quite elaborate, whereas at many other places they are brief and merely indicative.

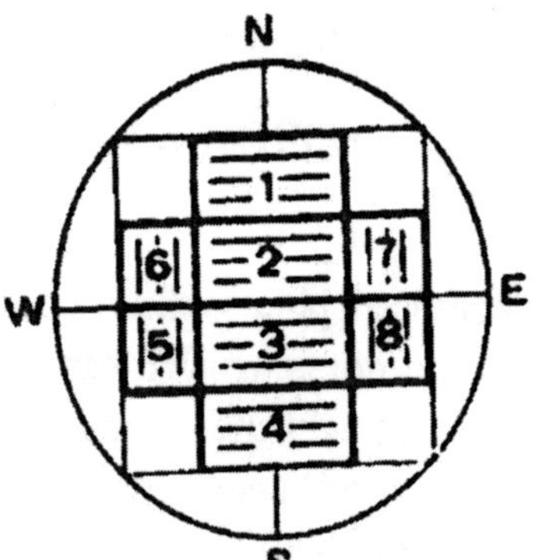

Fig. I : Garnapatya Hearth (Eggeling)

Baudhayana while describing the construction of various altars, deals with a number. of postulates in connection with the division of figures such as straight lines, rectangle, circle and triangle. These are real signs of geometrical operation. These postulates include :-

I. Dividing a circle into a number of parts.
II. Bisecting the diagonal of a rectangle.
III. To show that the diagonals of a rhombus bisects each other at right angle.
IV. Dividing a triangle into a number of equal similar parts.
V. Constructing a parallelogram at rectangle on same base and within the same parallel to show the equality of area etc.

In case of the Baudhyana sutra, there is a reference that Dhisnya be a sphere of circle in shape and it is divided into 9 equal parts. When it is circular, it describes a small circle above the centre and the annuals into 8 equal parts by dividing in diameters etc. This is nothing but dividing a circle into a number of parts by drawing diameters.

PYTHEGOREAN THEOREM WAS DISCOVERED BY BAUDHAYANA

Known after a Greek philosopher, Pythagoras (540 B.C.) the theorem of Phythagoras which means that the sphere of each rectangle side of a right angle triangle is equal to sphere of the diagonal. This means that the diagonal of the rectangle produces both (areas) with its length and produce separately. This is what the Baudhayana had enunciated. This means that the area of the sphere described on the diagonal of the sphere

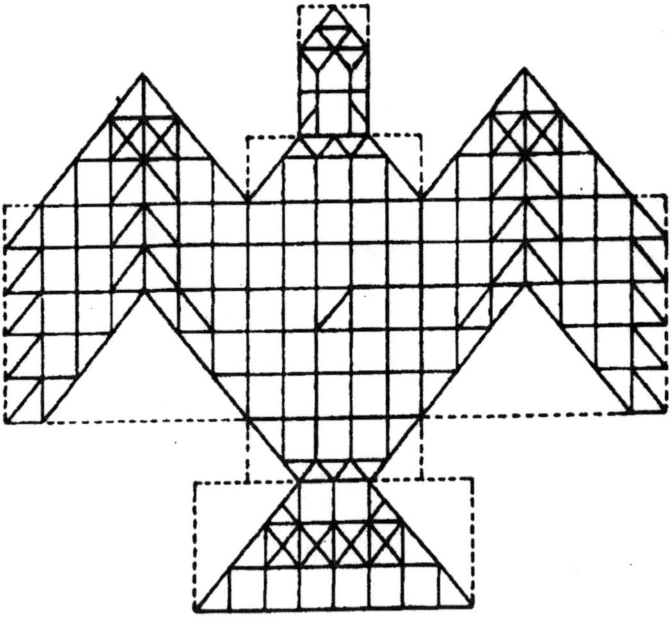

Fig. 2 : Caturasra Syena-cit.

is double the area of that square. Baudhyana theorem of sphere of diagonal is well illustrated in the construction of the KATURASRA SYENA-CIT as discovered by Burk. Caturasra Syena-Cit is very notable Fire-altar of the shape of falcon with curved wings and out spread tail the details of which have been given in Baudhayana Sulbha Sutra (translated by Thihant). The altar utilizes 200 bricks in all.

The sphere ACFE on the diagonal AC of the sphere ABCD of the four sphere forming the atman of this altar is obviously equal to the sphere EADEH on the side AD and sphere DGEH on the side DC.

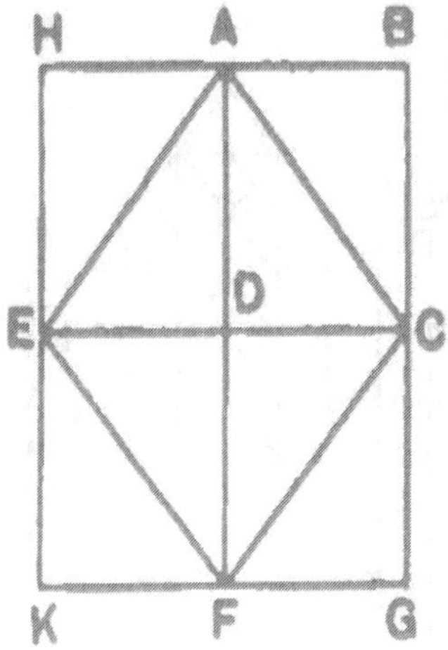

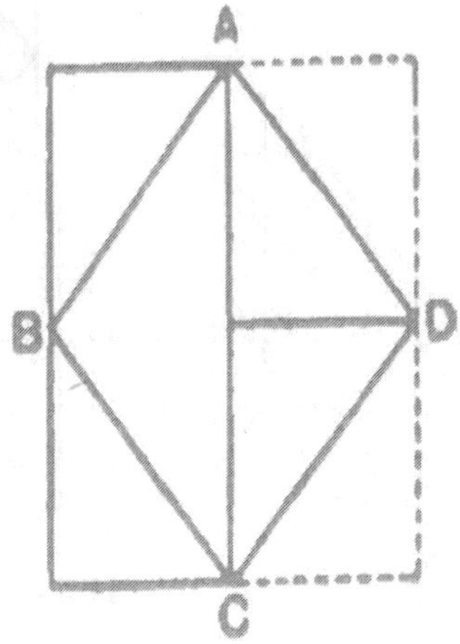

CONTRIBUTION OF BAUDHAYANA

The contribution of Baudhayana as a great geometer of ancient India is very significant. The pythagaurus theorem as square of diagonals goes to his credit and infact it should be rightly called as Baudhayana theorem as it was he who demonstrated the truth for the first time and gave its application. Baudhayana has not given the proof of the theorem. However, we join with Trihaut in the following words.

"The authors of the Sutras do not give us any hint as to the way in which they found their proposition regarding the diagonal of a square, but we suppose that they, too, were observant of the fact that the square of the diagonal is divided by its own diagonals into four triangles one of which is equal to half the first square. This is at the same time an immediately convincing proof of the Pythagorean proposition as far as squares or equilateral rectangular triangles are concerned".

As has already been mentioned, the science of geometry developed around the yajnas in construction of Vedis of various shapes. As such the development of the geometry took place here without having been borrowed from other countries. Following is the brief of contribution of Baudhayana to the science of geometry :

I. To give postulates of geometrical construction comprising of various geomertrical operations.

II. To discover the theorem of square of the diagonal called as Pythagaurus Theorem.

III. To determine accurately the value of under root 2 and to give the concept of irrationality of construction.

It may however, be mentioned that Baudhayana was not the first to discover all the geometrical concepts mentioned in his SULBA SUTRA and surely Rigveda, Taiteeraya Sanhita and Satpatha Brahmna have provided the same guidance to the matter but it is sure that he was a great teacher. He was the first teacher whose writings have influenced many Acharyas of Ancient India for centuries like Apastamba, Katyayana, Manu etc.

BAUDHYANA

AT A GLANCE

Age & Birth

Age Around 500-300 B.C.

Important Works

- *Baudhyana Sulbha Sutra containing Geometrical Construction, and Geometrical principles.*
- *Theorem of the square of Signifiant Contribution Diagonal (Pythagoras Theorem)*
- *Determined accurately the value of under roots 2.*

11

Salihotra
The Father of Veterinary Science

11

SALIHOTRA - THE FATHER OF VETERINARY SCIENCE

In ancient India, wars were fought riding on the back of horses and elephants. The huge army maintained by kings and rulers would comprise of several thousands of horses, elephants etc. Megasthenese (Greek ambassador in India) who was a courtier of Chandergupta, furnishes an account of Maurya Empire according to which there were nearly a lakh of horses and elephants looked after well.

The victory or defeat in war would depend much on the health of horses and elephants who were given special training for the purpose by the coach master and were provided special food. After the conclusion of war the injured animals had to be treated adequately and fully. It is therefore no surprise that in Mahabharata this was a subject of study for a king called "Ashwa Chikitsa" which means treatment of horses. Nakula and Sahdeva of the five Pandavas were well versed in this art and Guru Darona provided them special training on seeing their aptitude in veterinary science. During the last year of their forest exile Nakula and Sehdeva accepted the job of tending of horses and elephants of king Virate as per the great epic of Mahabharata and shown their expertise in this science and art.

Charioteering was considered a respectable profession in Ancient India where in the chariots were drought by horses and the warriors would fight wars riding on chariots.

Lord Krishna agreed to be the Charioteer of Arjuna in Mahabharta – the fieriest war of ancient India and for a Chariot, the training of Veterinary Science was very important. As such in ancient, India development of Veterinary Science took place from very early times to treat horses and elephants. The ancient works in Ayurveda like Charak Samhita, Susruta Samhita have specific mention on treatment of horses. Matsya and Garuda Puranas contained separate chapter on the care of sick animals.

Evidence is not lacking to show that there were competent physicians specialised in the treatment of animals and Salihotra stands fore most among them whose name had become synonymous to animal physician particularly of horses.

AGE AND BIRTH OF SALIHOTRA

Like many other scientists of ancient India the exact date and place of birth of Salihotra is not precisely known. However, he is said to have lived at Sravasti near Baharich district in U.P. While according to some other sources he belonged to Salatur near Kandhar. His father's name is mentioned as Hayaghosa - Brahmmsage. As regards the age of Salihotra he has been described as contemporary to Agnivasa and has been mentioned as the pupil of the same teacher thereby suggesting that Salihotra lived around 8th century B.C.

WORKS AND CONTRIBUTION OF SALIHOTRA

Haya Aurveda which is also called as Salihotra Samhita is the most outstanding works on disease and treatment of horses and is attributed to Salihotra which is a comprehensive treatise on the subject and was considered as standard work in ancient time on horses and no other work of earlier times can surpass the Haya Ayurvda of Salihotra in many a respects. Not only the many Puranas composed subsequently contain chapters of the treatise but it was translated in many a foreign languages being full of knowledge in the diagnosis and treatment of horses.

SALIHOTRA

AT A GLANCE

Age And Birth

Around 8th Century B.C, lived in Sravasti(Gonda & Bahrai Distt. in UP.

Important Works

- *Haya Ayurveda a compendiusu.*
- *Dealing with Care and Treatment of horses*

12

Kanada

A Great Atomic Scientist- Philosopher

12

KANADA : A GREAT ATOMIC SCIENTIST-PHILOSOPHER

In today's world atom bomb, nuclear bomb, hydrogen bomb and other new kind of nuclear devices are well-known and are considered to be the product of modern science. The first explosion of atom bomb by US took the world by surprise and made devastation to such a horrible extent that the cities of Hiroshima and Nagasaki of Japan became the graveyard of thousands and millions of people. The world was amazed to see the tremendous and unprecedented power of atom bombs.

It will however, be unbelievable that the concept of atom and the atomic theory in ancient way is the product of our great ancient scientists which was treated as philosophy but was true in regard to the concept of atom. Kanada is the first such great atomic scientist of ancient India. It is interesting to mention that there was no demarcation in ancient India between what we now call religion, philosophy and science and all these disciplines were utilized to explore the fundamental truth.

This amalgamation of different aspects of knowledge led many foreign scholars to attach no significance to the scientific theories contained in them. It is only after we rid ourselves of this bias, come to the conclusion that the scientific theories therein, though not based upon regular experiments in the laboratory are worthy of consideration. This also holds good in case of Kanada.

The age of Kanada is believed somewhere around 600 B.C., however, his works were appreciated only in the 20th century and professor A.B. Keith in his book on Indian Logic and Atomism published in 1921 gave an excellent account of some of the main thoughts developed in regard to the concept of matter and atomic theory of Kanada. Though, in the sacred books of Hindu's series, an English translation of the Sutras of Kanada and commentary of Sankara Misra was published in the year 1911.

BIRTH AND AGE OF KANADA

The expounder of atomic theory is known by various names such as Aulukya, Kasyap and the more popular one - Kanada, whose treatise named as Vaisesika consists of 10 books, each of 2 chapters. From the various names by which Kanada is known, it transpires that he was the son of Uluka, a highly spiritual family of Kasyapa. As per "Modern Reveal" 1909, he belonged to Prabhasa[1] in Allahabad district and his

1. तदाप्यहं भविष्यामि सोमशर्मा द्विजोत्तमः।
प्रभासतीर्थमासाद्य योगात्मा लोकविश्रुतः ॥२०२॥
तत्रापि मम न पुत्रा भविष्यन्ति तपोधनाः।
अक्षपादः कणादश्च उलूको वत्स एव च॥२०३॥
— *Vayu Purana, Purva, Chapter 23*

teacher was Som Sarma and as per Puranas, he was regarded as incarnation of Lord Siva. Kanada lived the life of an ascetic and used for his daily bread, particle of rice scattered on public streets. As he would feed on particles, i.e. Kanas, he was known as Kanada, Kanabhaksa or Kanabhuk.[2]

As the story goes, Kanada pleased Lord Shiva- the grand master of learning who delivered learning the truth contended in it, appointed him to compose a compendium.

THE VAISISIKA SUTRA

Kanada's sutras of Vaisesika system find reference in many ancient works like Vayu purana, Padam purana, Devi Bhagwati, Maha Bharta and other scriptures which indicate that the sutras were very popular at that time. The Vashasika system of Kanada finds mention in vedant sutras also which shows that the former were composed earlier to Mahrishi Vayas who is called the author of Vedanta.[3]

---

2. The word Kanada has been otherwise interpreted by some as meaning Atom-eater, and it is suggested that the author of the Vaisesika-Sutras is called by that name because he has propounded the theory of atoms.

3. (i) महद् दीर्घवद्वा ह्रस्वपरिमण्डलाभ्याम्।
(ii) उभयथापि न कर्मातस्तदभावः।
(iii) समवायाभ्युपगमाच्च साम्यादनवस्थितेः।
(iv) नित्यमेव च भावात्।
(v) रूपादिमत्त्वाच्च विपर्ययो, दर्शनात्।
(vi) उभयथा च दोषात्।
(vii) अपरिग्रहाच्चात्यन्तमनपेक्षा।

— *Veds. 11.2.11-17*

In view of the above evidences, it could be concluded that Vaisesika is the oldest of all systems of Vedic Philosphy and was composed by Kanada and it is the first systematic work of Vaisesika Philosophy belonging to 6th century B.C.

ATOMIC THEORY OF KANADA AND ATOM BOMB

Kanada is the first expounder of atomic theory which is based upon the existence of real things in the universe. The Vaisesika sutra of Kanada consists of 10 books and each book has 2 chapters, the total sutras being 370 as details given below.

Book	I	II	III	IV	V	VI	VII	VIII	IX	X
No. of Sutras	31	31	19	13	18	16	28	6	13	9

The Vaisesika Darsan is one of the well-known six systems of the Vedic philosophy. However, the later development of atomic theory is the product of Nyaya Vaisesika School contributed by Gotama and Kanada.

A number of commentaries on this system are available. The Prasastapada Bhasya, also known as Padartha-dharmasamggrahs is one of the very well-known books of the Vaisesika School. Sankara Misra wrote a notable commentary on the Vaisesika known as Upaskara.

ATOMIC THEORY OF KANADA

Kanada has divided the universe under six categories as under –

1. Drayva (substance)
2. Guna (Quality)
3. Karma i.e. action
4. Samanya means belonging or generality or coordination
5. Visesa means particular
6. Sameyaya which relates to the relation to the constituent part.

Kanada has subdivided the substances into following entities namely :

(i) Earth (ii) Water (iii) Fire or heat (iv) Air (v) Time (vi) Space, besides mind and soul.

It may be noted that these substances are not to be taken in their superficial form but in term of their composition. The earth represents all substances which are solid. Similarly water and air will denote liquid and gas substances. These are composed of different kinds of parmanus. Akash i.e. ether, dik i.e. space and kala which means time have been mentioned as eternal and pervading and are inseparable substances. The origin and destruction of objects of the world has been explained through combination and separation of Pramanus.

Parmanu (Atom), according to Kanada is the smallest part of a substance and everything in the universe is made of parmanus, and no further division is possible of a parmanu. In fact, it is the ultimate particle of each of 4 entitled substances earth, fire, water and air. Such a particle is necessarily super sensuous. However, it does not imply its non-existence and it may be due to the action of certain factors which stand in its way of perception. The important characteristics of atoms are:

i. Parmanu is the smallest/ultimate particle of substance of water, air, earth and fire. It is indivisible and incapable of further analysis.
ii. The parmanus of Earth Air, Fire and water have the essential attributes touch taste, smell and colour.
iii. There can be no visual perception of Parmanu and sense organs can not percieve them.
iv. They are eternal.
v. They are the ultimate material cause of the universe. Under the action of Teja (Heat) Parmanu undergo chemical change resulting into transformation of characterstics of Parmanu and reunion with different groups and configuration forming a new product with different properties.

The process of chemical change has been examplified by a raw earthen pot put into fire. Under the action of heat its colour, physical properties, strength all undergo change and the new product shows different properties.

Similarly, in the case of earthen bricks and the bricks burnt and baked in a kiln, a wide difference of properties takes place:

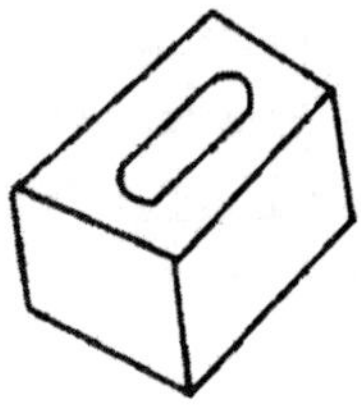

Raw Earth Brick
(Brittle, Colour, Grey)

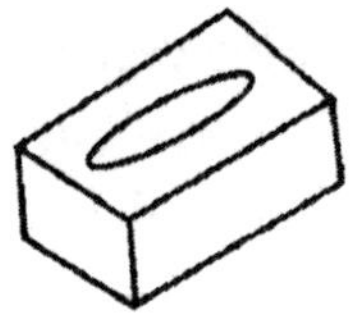

Burnt Brick
(Tough, Stronger Colour, Pale or red)

Uniting of Parmanus and formation of substances : The occurance of Parmanus and their uniting with each other and forming the substances have been expounded by Kanada as under.

1) Parmanu of a substance unites with another Parmanu to form Dvynuka which could be called molecule. The molecule have the same property as that of the original property of the Parmanu.

2) Parmanus may also unite in a group, two, three or four numbers (pairs, triads, teterads etc.)

3) The binary molecules i.e. Dvynukas may unite in pairs or by groups of three, four, five etc.

4) The aggregates thus formed create elementry substances. The qualities and properties of these aggregate Parmanus

remain the same as original Parmanus till no chemical change takes place under the action of teja.

COMPARISON WITH MODERN ATOMIC THEORY

The Atomic Theory of Kanada holds close comparison with the modern atomic theory. John Dalton, an English chemist, presented the Atomic Theory in the year 1808 and known as the founder of Theory of Atoms. According to this theory, matter is composed of atoms and an atom is the smallest particle of matter which cannot be sub-divided further. Atoms of same element were said to have similar properties like mass, volume. Also that atoms combine in a definite proportion to form compound atoms.

KANADA

Age and Birth

Around 600 B.C. at Prabhasa in Allahabad distt.

Important Works

- *Vaisesike Sutra*
- *The first systematic work of vaisesike philosophy.*

Achievements

- *Expounder of theory of Atoms*
- *Has remarkable similarity with modern theory of Atom.*

13

Susurta

The Father of Surgery

13

SUSURTA
THE FATHER OF SURGERY

"In both branches of the Aryan stock, surgical practice (as well as medical) reached a high degree of perfection at a very early period."

Encyclopaedia Britannica
by Chales Creighton.

"The whole plastic surgery in Europe took a new flight when these cunning devices of Indian workmen became known to us."

Dr. Hirschberg of Berlin.

These are the compliments made by international authorities on ancient Indian surgery for which the credit goes to Susruta who is regarded as father of ancient Indian surgery.

Susruta lived somewhere in 6th century B.C. It was he, who from scanty material created science of surgery in methodical order inviting the admiration of the world even after thousands of years of human history of surgery known as 'Susruta shalya Tantra' composed around 6th century B.C. which contains a systematic account of the surgical experiences of old surgeons by collecting the scattered facts of the science from the vast range of the vedic literature.

DEVELOPMENT OF SURGERY IN ANCIENT INDIA :

Surgery like many other sciences developed around the yajna i.e. fire sacrifice. It was Susurta who first classified all surgical operations into eight different kinds and grouped them under various heads and yajna became a centre of anatomical surgery.

Before the age of Susurta neither physician nor the surgeon were beholden in great respect and physicians had to go out into the eopen streets calling out the patients like hawkers. As regards surgery they were considered as second to the physicians. In fact, origin of surgery, was the result of the necessity when the arrows piercing into the bodies of warriors had to be taken out. We find mention of the amputation of legs of warriors. During peace time surgery became necessary for the cases of accidents and for the injuries sustained by the rich and poor.

Susruta was not only the surgeon of versatile personality, but he was a teacher of surgical instrument technology as well as metallurgy.

BIRTH AND IDENTITY OF SUSURTA

Susurta has been mentioned to be the son of Vishwamitra the great sage of vedic period though being Akshtray king he rose to the divine level of Rishi. Mahabharta mentions the name of several sons of Vishwamitra which includes Susurta also. It appears that Vishwamitra while foresaking his kingdom and devoting himself in tapsya sent his son Susurta to a high learned king Diyodas for being imparted the knowledge of Ayurveda.

AGE OF SUSURTA SANHITA

It is difficult to ascertain the age of Susurta Sanhita as the original book is not available to us at present. We have only a revised version made by Nagarjuna, an eminent Buddhist philosopher as well as medical scientist. According to some of the authorities (Hass and John Willson) Susurta Sanhita was written much after Mahabharta and the consensus of western opinion is to place NagaArjuna in the first quarter of 300 B.C. and the final recession of Sanhita by NagaArjuna thereafter. In view of the fact that Susurta has been mentioned by Katyana (400 B.C.) in his work Vartika, the original Sanhita was written before the birth of Lord Buddha.

ACHIEVEMENTS OF SUSURTA

SURGERY

Susurta devoted his life for the cause and performance of surgery and his achievements could be briefed as under:

1. Pre-requisites for performing surgery procedure and new modern techniques.

2. Plastic Surgery and Modern Technique. Performing surgery like amputation, fracture, Harnia, rupture and other such operations with sophiscated techniques.
3. Ophthalmic surgery.
4. Midwifery.
5. Details of instruction in anatomy and surgery.
6. Management and pre-requisite in surgery.

1. **Surgery Procedure** - Susruta laid down the details regarding management of patients before surgery, requirements of operation room etc. As per Susurta-Sanhita if surgery is to be performed in mouth, patient should be kept on fasting and for abdominal surgery, a light refreshment should be given. For operation room, antiseptic treatment should be given and the chamber should be falugated with the vapours of white mastard, nimha leaves etc. He even devised a method of anaesthesia.

2. **Plastic Surgery and modern technique** - The achievements in case of plastic surgery are wonderful. The transplantation of sensible skin flesh by mending it clipt earloped with a patch of sensible skin, skinflex from somewhere the part of the body were the devices which were not even known to the modern plastic surgery for quite long time back and perhaps the method devised by Susruta have influenced the modern surgery *to adopt* the same with usual refixed units and amendments. He described a method for fixing a neve new where it had been cut off.

3. **Amputation and abdominal operations** :- Susruta evolved a wonderful method of joining the intestinal wombs by letting big ants bite the cut ends of the intestines which had been brought nearer to head and then cutting off the body of the ants leaving only the heads of the ants which acts a clamp and well tolerated by the body. In fact it serves the purpose of animal tissue which the modern surgery uses. This method was later on followed by the Arabs and other countries. In warfare which was fought with arrows, Susruta mentioned the use of certain medical plasters to be applied to localise the sharp arrows and thereby identifying the exact location of embedding of arrows. For amputation of limbs the necessity of aneathesetic drugs was realized and wine was used to serve the purpose.

4. **Difficult surgical Operations**: - Susruta performed all types of the operation like fracture, dislocation, harnia, fisstula, removal of foreign bodies etc. involving excision, incision, puncture and other such processes.

5. The genius and surgery skill of Susruta becomes crystal clear in the field of midwifery. Susrutasanhita describes the handling and applications of forceps besides attempting, turning, flexing and glidding movements.

He also tried the caesareass operation in hopeless cases where the maternal passage is not compatible to the child. The requirements of the labour room in the absence of hospital were also prescribed.

6. **Instructions in Practical Surgery and Anatomy: -** Susruta laid down the procedure and method to pursue the study of practical surgery and practical Anatomy, he mentions that a learner should try the knives first on virtual and artificial objects, and how the bandaging is to be learnt etc. For study of practical anatomy the sacrificial animals in yajnas were to be used for the purpose which was perhaps permissible in those days.

Susruta is in favour of 300 bones against 360 bones recognised by vedic traditions. Of those 120 are found in the fore extremities, 170 in the palmist, side back, chest abdomn etc. and rest in the region of neck. It is where the Susurt Sanhita contains anomaly and this may be on account of the fact that the original Susurtsanhita has passed through several recensions. However, the Susurtsanhita has described the union of bones and ligaments nerves, brawins etc. in a wonderful and correct manner.

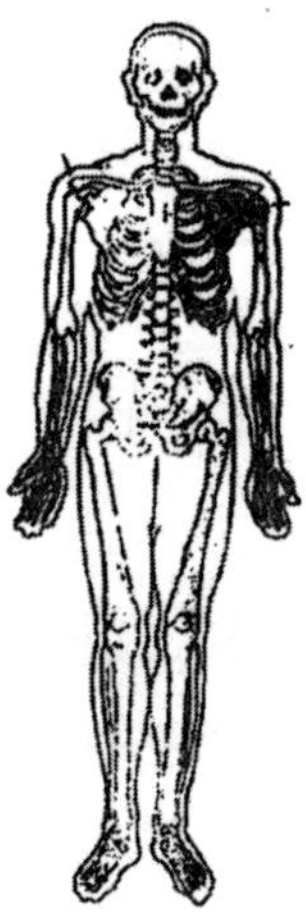

Susruta as surgical instrument technologist : In modern surgery surgeons are only aware with the use and handling of surgical instruments during the performance of operation and they are not concerned with the metallurgy, manufacturing and other requirements which is a job of technologist. Susruta describes more than 100 surgical instruments made of steel and the composition of the metal has also been given. The requirement of these instruments have been mentioned that they should have good handles and firm joints, be well polished, and sharp enough to divide a hair. They should be perfectly clean, and kept in flannel in a wooden box. They included various wshapes of scalpels, bistouries, lancets, scarifiers was, bone-nippers, sciessors, trocars, and needles. There were also blunt hooks, loops, probes (including a caustic holder), directors, sounds, scoops, and forceps (for polypi etc.), as well as catheters, syringes, a rectal speculum and bougies.

The following description on surgical instrument will show that Susruta was possessed of deep knowledge of metallurgy and instrument technology :

"Instruments that are fitted with handles of easy grip and are made of good and pure iron, well-sharp, and are set with edges that are not jagged and end in well-formed points or tops, should be deemed as the best of their kind."

Curvature, bluntness (kuntha-Lit : incapable of cutting hair), unequal sharpness of the edge, roughness and over-shortness are the defective traits in a surgical instrument. Those possessed of contrary features should be used. But A Karapatram set with a very rough (dentated) edge may be used for the purpose of sawing the bones.

A surgical instrument meant for excision (Bhedanam) should be set with an edge as thin as that of a Masura pulse (lentill seed), while an instrument used in scraping should be set with an edge half as thin as that of the former. An instrument used either in connection with the measures of secretion or cutting by uplifting (Vyadhanam) should be set with an edge as fine as the human hair, while an instrument of incision should have an edge half as that of the former.

Surgical instruments should be tempered with one of the tree substances such as alkali, water, and oil. Instruments used in cutting an arrow, a bone or any foreign matter (salyam) pricked into the human body should be tempered with alkali, whereas those that are used in cutting, cleaving and lopping off the flesh from an affected part, should be tempered with water . Instruments used in opening (Vyuadhanam) a vain (sira) or in cutting open a nerve (snayu) should be tempered with oil and should be whetted upon a species of stone slab resembling a Masa pulse in colour, and their set-edge should be protected by putting it in a sheatmade of Salmal i wood.

An instrument, well-shaped, fitted with a convenient handle and capable of (literally) spliting a hair in two and made according to measures laid down in the Sastras, should be alone used in a surgical operation.

SUSURTA - AS TEACHER

Susruta not only practised surgery but taught surgery as well. The pupil who received training in surgery as apprentices must have become good surgeon later on. The adequate material contained in Susruta is a clear testimony to support the fact. Susruta asked their students to try their knives repeatedly first on certain virtual as well as artificial objects before undertaking the actual operation and vegetables were used as practising material by the pupil for various surgical procedures such as incision making. The other kinds of stuff such as dummies and dead animals were also used. Different types of sutures and ligatures for clothes and bandaing on dummies were practiced. Since the actual surgery was to be performed on human bodies as such dead bodies on which dissections were to be performed and to be demonstrated were first kept covered with grass in the flowing water of the river. The muscles, internal organs and bones were studied after the skin has been peeled off. Susruta was well conscious of the fact that practical training is very much necessary for surgery. Therefore he stressed upon the importance of the same. His views are clearly brought out in Sanhita when he remarks :

"The physician who has learnt only bookish knowledge (bastras) but is unacquainted with the practical methods of treatment or the one who knows the practical details of the treatment but from self-confidence does not study the books is unfit to practice his profession. Such person deserves to be killed by the king".

MEDICAL BOTANY

The ayurvedic drugs and medicines are based upon herbs. A herbal garden for growing medicinal plants is desirable. This has also attracted the attention of Susruta who has given a detailed description of the medicinal plants and the soil best suited for their growth. Since the plant growing in a plot of land are also influenced with the property of soil on which it grow, the characterties of the ground best suited for the planting of medicinal herbs and trees are mentioned. He has given the requirement of the surface of the ground and has also mentioned that the ground chosen for plant should have not been a site of cremation or garbage dumps etc. The characteristics of the soil has been mentioned which according to Susruta should be glossary firm, steady, black, yellowish or red but free from sand, potash or other alkaline substances.

SUSRUTA AS MEDICAL METALLURGIST

This is one of the aspect of the versatile knowledge and genious of Susruta to have described the properties and uses of various metals and their compounds. In fact he has given the uses from the point of medicine and not from the consideration of metallurgy. In view of the fact that the uses of metals is important in ayurveda, Susruta has given the properties of such metals. Silver has been described to be laxative, destroying bile and wind but acidic taste. Zinc and lead has been stated as destroyer of worms in the body and of saline taste. Copper is corrosive, laxative in its potency, has sweet and astringent taste. Gold has many good properties from the medicine point of view. It is a tonic and balances the deranged humours of the body, it invigorates the eye sight and is cooling and antitoxic. It possesses a sweet and agreeable taste. The properties of pearls, corals, diamonds, sapphires, have also been mentioned from the point of view of the application in ayurvedic medicines.

SUSURTA

The Father of Surgery

AT A GLANCE

Age & Birth

6th century B.C, place of birth controversial

Important Works

- *Susurta Shalya Tantra*

Achievements

- *Surgery procedure and new modern techniques.*
- *Plastic surgery and other surgery like amputation, fracture, hernia etc.*
- *Ophthalmic surgery*
- *Anatomy and surgery*
- *Norms for surgical instrument*
- *Teaching system in surgery*
- *Medical botany*
- *Medical metallurgist*

14

Nagarjuna

A Scholar, A Scientist
A Metallurgist

14

NAGARJUNA
A SCHOLAR, A SCIENTIST
A METALLURGIST

"Holy bank of river Ganges, near Patli putra, Hermitage made of bushes and wild grass; A lean and thin personality with no clothing around chest and head is busy in writing on Bhoj Patra in the dim light of twinkling earthen lamps in evening hours. The mighty king Kanishka accompanied by his scholar minister Ashaughosha are standing at the door step of the hermitage to have meeting with the lean man inside".

This is one of the true portrait of Nagarjuna who was reckoned as a top ranking philosopher, an eminent Buddhist scholar, a scientist, a technologist and a metallurgist par excellence.

The land of Vidharbha has the singular distinction to have given birth to Archarya Nagarjuna in 7-8 B.C. in a high and respected Brahmin family at Chhatisgarh. In those days Vidharbha was also known as south Kaushal and the same has been mentioned by Hiuen-Tsang, the famous Chinese traveller as the birth place of Nagarjuna. As per tradition prevailing in those days Nagarjuna made a thorough study of Vedas and vedangas at Patilputra which was a famous centre of learning, on the holy bank of River Ganges. Nagarjuna pursued the study under the pupilage of a competent Acharya since the age of 18 years. He made serious and concentrated study of Ayurveda and Buddhist philosophy. After having completed his study and with the blessing of his teachers. Nagarjun settled in a hermitage constructed at the bank of river at Gaya, which was a historical place. Many a philosophical works and treatises like Suhnllkha and Madhnic were written at this very hermitage High ranking scholars, experts of philosophy were all the time rallying around Nagarjun whose fame of scholarliness and knowledge was not only limited to Vidharbha and Gaya but to the entire country of India. History is silent to divulge as to who were the fortunate parents to have given birth to Nagarjun whose fame was touching the sky and there was no assembly or conference without the name of Nagarjun. The mightly king Kanishka was much influenced with Buddhism and accompanied with his Prime minister went to meet Nagarjun. The rays of the fame of Nagarjun found its way in the royal Darbar of King Satavahana who made Nagarjun as his envoy but even after being Rajguru, his living was not a grand palace but a hut or Ashram situated at the bank of river Krishna.

Three Nagarjunas **:** The study of various works and excerpts reveals that there have been more than one person with the name of Nagarjuna in different periods. Albureni has mentioned a personality with the name of Nagarjuna who has been a century before his arrival in India i.e. in 700 A.D. who was an expert with excellence in the science of chemistry. On the other hand Hiuen-T. Sang-the Chinese traveller has also mentioned of a scholar with the name of Nagarjun who was capable to convert stone into gold. Again a famous work 'Rajtarangi' mentions that a great scholar with the name of Acharya Nagarjun has been 150 years after Lord Buddha. Thus, there had been three persons with the name of Nagarjun as under:

i) *Nagarjuna* of the period 150 years before (Lord Buddha mentioned in 'Rajtarnagini'.

ii) *Nagarjuna* as mentioned by Hiuen-T. Sang having been in first century A.D.

iii) *Nagarjuna* of 7th century A.D. as mentioned by Alberuni.

The meaningful details regarding first Nagarjun are not available in Rajtarangini except that he was Buddhist king. As regards the second Nagarjun, Hiuen-Tsang is clear to mention that he was Buddhist scholar and was capable to convert the stone into gold through the science of chemistry and he was very close friend as well as guru of king Shatvahan. In a very ancient book by Shatvahan's charioteer written on Bhojpatra, Nagarjuna has been mentioned as guru of king Shatvahan. It is mentioned that the Gupta rulers got the medical prescriptions given by Nagarjun engraved on pillars. The mention of Rahul Sanskritayana, the famous Buddhist monk also confirms that

Nagarjun was born in Vidharbh in South India and he was a disciple of Aashvghosha. As regards the Nagarjun which have been mentioned by Alberuni belonging to seventh century, nothing is known about his birth antencedants and its is possible that Alberuni without thorough investigations might have mentioned Naga arjun belonging to 7th century. However, it is difficult to say anything clearly and categorically.

Nagarjuna had written several books of high order and many of them are the treatise on philosophy, tantrism and spiritualism. The subject of some of the books is medical science. Works on metallurgy are also being attributed to Nagarjun. In nutshell, the works of Nagarjuna may be classified as under :

(i) Philosophy (ii) Tantrism

(iii) Medical science (iv) Metallurgy

The main books on Buddhist philosophy are nearly 20 and were translated by Kumarjiva in the year 405 A.D. On tantric science the main books include Tatav Parakash, Param Rahisya Sukabhi, Sambodhi, Samay Mudra etc.

Nagarjun has written an original and independent book on Opthamalogy which is known under the title 'Yen lung'. This book deals with the disease of eye treatment and diagnose on eye ailments. Yet one more book 'Adhishastra' the subject of which. Genetic science was also written by Nagarjun. One book on metallurgy, yet another book on Lohsastra (science of metals) is mentioned to have been written by Nagarjuna which, unfortunately is not available. Nagarjun has made a number of experiments on metals as well as medicines and it has been mentioned in 'Harash Charhita'. He presented two compendium of Rata Mala and Rashyan Gutika to the king Shatvahan which shows his science genious.

CONTRIBUTION MADE BY NAGARJUNA

Philosophy

Nagarjun was a distinguished philosopher and was contemporary to Asuaghosa, Aryadev and Kumaralabha who have been called four illuminating sun by Hiuen-Tsang. It was he who formulated the dotrine of the void (sunya or tathata) in his famous Madhyamika-sastra, which has won him a lasting place in world philosophy. In the same work he also distinguished between two truths, the conventional truth and the highest truth, without which it is not possible to understand either the void or Nirvana, which are matters not of intellectual grasp but of intuitive wisdom (Prajna). Other important works attributed to Nagarjuna are the Satasa harsrikaprajnaparamita, the Dasabhumi-vibhasa-sastra, and the Suhrillekha. I-Tsing speaks in high terms of the last work and observes that in his days it was widely read and memorized in India. Nagarjuna later became head of the University of Nalanda, and was succeeded there by his famous disciple Aryadeva, who was of Sinhalese origin. Aryadeva preached Buddhism for sometime in Prayaga, where he showed great courage in condemning the superstition of the multitude thronging to bathe in the river through his most famous work in Chatuh-Sataka. According to Winternitz, down to the present day, Nagarjuna's Madhyamika Sastra, together with Aryadeva's Chatuh-Sataka or Sata-Sastra, and the Dvadas-nikaya Sastra, form the groundwork of the faith of the sanron sect in Japan. All through the works of the famous trio, Asvaghosa, Nagarjuna and Aryadeva, the early patriarchs of the Mahayana, worship of the Buddha and absolute surrender (saranagati) for him are ardently expressed, along with the various metaphysical doctrines, as the key-notes of the new system of faith.

NAGARJUNA AS METALLURGIST AND ALCHEMIC:

The age of Nagarjuna was dominant with experiments on metals and mercury. He proved the uses of mercury by conducting hundreds of experiments in his laboratory and was successful to discover the wonderful power of mercury. As per Vag Bhatt, one of the mercury was of red colour which was most useful for alchemic purposes and was capable even to make the man almost immortal. The other kind of mercury was of light grey colour which was used by the people of Nag Desha against ageing. However, on account of invasions of foreigners, the sources of mining of red and grey mercury were closed down. Nagarjuna has written a number of scientific books one of which 'Yogsatak' has been published. One more work "Chitanand Patiasee" has been found in Tibet written on Bhoj Patra and it is not possible to give the complete account of the books Nagarjun wrote on the subject. Hiuen T-sang a famous Chinese traveller has mentioned Nagarjuna to be an expert in chemistry science and capable to convert stone into gold and this proves that Nagarjuna made unique discovery regarding various metals and mercury. These experiments relate not only to mercury but many other compounds of metals, sub-metals and non-metals.

The laboratory of Nagarjuna has been mentioned to be located at 'Sri Parvat' and there was a good collection of metal and submetals procured from far and wide. It has also been mentioned in certain works that many metals were imported from China, Greek, Tapti river etc. and various minerals were divided as : Rush Raj, Mha Rush Up Rush and Simple Rush. It has also been stated that Nagarjuna was aware as to which mercury could be converted into gold. A famous work 'Rush Ratanakar' has been written by Nagarjuna. It is, however not clear that this was the work of first Nagarjuna or second Nagarjuna or the last. Perusal of book shows the wonderful work done on the subject. It may be mentioned that there had been 27 experts and scientists of mercury and the detailed list of the names have been given in 'Ras Ratna Smuchy'. Out of this long list there are only four prominent names :

1. Nandi
2. Naga Arjuna
3. Munishwara
4. Som Deva

According to Veg Bhatt there have been no scholar of the science of Rasa more competent than the four names. In addition to these, there have been nearly 19 more scholars in the science of Rasa, however, Naga Arjuna surpasses all.

NAGARJUNA AS MEDICAL SCIENTIST

The unique contribution of Nagarjuna on the subject, is to write commentary on Susrut Sanhita and he made number of improvements therein. It may be mentioned that upto the period of Susrut Sanhita, though the various acharyas of Ayurveda were able to discover the usefulness of organic and in-organic elements and metals, however, Nagarjuna speltout the good uses of mercury as medicine and and as the unique power to cure various diseases more than all the organic and inorganic metals. On hundreds of diseases he proved the curing power of mercury in various forms. He has also been mentioned to have written an independent and original book on eye diseases dealing the subject of ophthalmology completely. Similarly on genetic science also he has written independent book.

NAGAARJUNA

AT A GLANCE

Age And Birth

Around 7th –8th B.C, Chattisgarh

Important Works

- *Over 20 books on Medical Science, Metallurgy, Philosophy, Tantries* ***contribution*** *of Nagaarjuna*
- *Formulated Doctrine of void(Philosophy)*
- *Discovered wonderful power of Mercury.*
- *Scholar of Science of Rasa.*
- *Compiled final version of Susrut Sanita*

15

Jivaka
The Most Distinguished Physician

15

JIVAKA THE MOST DISTINGUISHED PHYSICIAN

A heap of old garbage with grown up bushes and weeds along side a road of Raj garhiya (near modern Patna) surrounded by a crowd of people.

The royal convoy of prince Abhay son of king Bimbsara passes along. A noise like jivata is prevading over. The prince noticing the crowd orders his attendant to go and see to 'what was the matter', who returns to the prince and reports "Some unclaimed baby appears to have been born 3 hrs earlier, is lying with scanty clothes and still alive. Prince Abhay orders the baby to be brought to him and the latter is taken under his own care."

This unclaimed baby later on became a famous Ayurvedic physician of ancient India between 5th and 6th century B.C. and was named as Jivaka by the king who earned such a name and fame during the period that patients from all over India would come to him for consultation and examination. Budhha also took treatment from him.

Jivaka who had been under the care of prince Abhaya came to hear about Takshila which was the famous centre of learning in those days for all technical arts.

Jivaka having determined to become a physician left for Takshila without informing anybody and got the pupilage of a famous Acharya of Ayurvedic medicine and studied for 7 years.

UNIQUE METHOD OF EXAMINATION

Jivaka on completion of seven years of his studies had to undergo a unique test, when his teacher asked him, "take this spade" said he "and seek a round of Takshila in yojana on every side and whatever plants you see which are not medicinal, bring it to me." Jivaka as a sincere and competent student walked round the city with spade in hand but every plant he examined was found to have some or the other medicinal use. He accordingly returned to his teacher to report the fact to him. The teacher was satisfied that his pupil did possess the requisite knowledge and he was permitted to go home to practice the medical science.

By this method it appears the teacher had satisfied himself that his pupil had imbibed the real knowledge of the medical science and he knew the use of every plant from the medicinal point of view which was a very important component of medical science in ancient India.

DIFFICULT CASES CURED

Jivaka successfully treated and cured many chronic diseases some of which are mentioned as under :-

A merchant's wife with chronic disease of head could not be cured by even world wide physicians was examined by Jivaka who administered medicated ghee through her nose which came out through her mouth and was spat out by the patient, this cured the patient immediately and as a reward 16,000 Kahapanas and servants and coach of horses were given to him.

Jivaka treated king Bimbsara, who was suffering from analfestula owing to which king was feeling miserable and was ridiculed and was made a laughing stock by his 500 wives. Jivaka took some ointment medicine on his finger and cured the king by just one application of the medicine on the affected part. The king was so happy that he gave fabulous ornaments of his wives and appointed Jivaka as royal physician.

SURGICAL OPERATIONS

Jivaka was not only an Ayurvedic physician but performed surgical operations also successfully. A merchant who was suffering from an acute head disease and was heading for death as per the physicians, was examined by Jivaka and a minor surgery was performed on the head of the patient, after cutting the skin he pulled out 2 worms which would otherwise have entered his brain in 2 days causing death to him. The patient was advised to lie on his left side, right side and back sides for seven months each in this position. However, the patient was cured, though he could lie for seven days only in each of the above position.

An abdominal surgery was performed by Jivaka in case of a male paient whose intestines got twisted by a gymnastic feat causing functional disorders of bowels and the patient was getting yellow and weak. With no surgical instruments and operation theatres available in those days, Jivaka tied the patient to a pillar and then cut through the skin belly and put the twisting intestines in correct position. Jivaka stitched the skin and applied ointment to heal the wound. This made the patient to restore to his normal health.

BUDDHA CURED WITHOUT MEDICINE

Jivaka was the physician of Lord Buddha and was also sincerely devoted to him. He would go to his Darshan daily when in town. Once Buddha fell ill due to the disturbance of humours as reported in Jatakas but would not take any medicine. Jivaka got the fat rubbed in his body for a few days and advised smelling of lotus leaves to have a mild purgative effect and thereafter take bath with warm water. Those measures cured Buddha completely without any medicine.

Many such instances show that he was one of the most eminent physicians of the time and people from far and wide would come to him for treatment. Many would embrace Buddhism simply to get treated by Jivaka. Lord Buddha placed him under the category of very good men among his followers. No doubt Jivaka was a shining star among ancient Indian physicians.

JIWAKA

AT A GLANCE

Age And Birth

Around 5th –6th B.C, birthplace at Rajgariha (near Patna)

Important Works

- *Incurable diseases of head cured*
- *King Bimbsara was cured of anus fishtoula*
- *Jaundice of Emperor of Avanti kingdom jaundice cured*
- *Abdomn operations-setting right the intestines done*
- *Buddha cured*

16

Charaka

An Ayurvedic Physician

16

CHARAKA
AN AYURVEDIC PHYSICIAN

Charaka is regarded as one of the pioneer of Ayurvedic medicine and is reckoned a great teacher of Ayurveda with excellence in the skill and science of Ayurveda. His name is so closely associated with Ayurveda that sometimes the two are used synonymous to each other.

BIRTH AND AGE OF CHARAKA

The exact age and birth of Charaka is a matter of controversy. According to European scholars, he was court physician to the king Kanishka of 2nd century A.D. Some of Hindu Scholars however, regard Charaka before Panini, the great grammarian of ancient India belonging to 6th century B.C. A common prevalent view, however, is that Charaka lived before 175 B.C. as Patanjali who belonged to this period, has written a commentary on the treatise of Charaka. Whatsoever may be the age and birth of Charaka, he is regarded by the classic authorities of Ayurvedic medicine as an incarnation of Ananta Shesa, the gaint cosmic Serpent, who supports this universe. The name Charaka has its origin from the word "CHARA", means a traveller and Charaka being a perapatic teacher went about from place to place to propagate the science of Ayurveda and acquired the name of

Charaka. During 7th & 8th centuries A.D. even the Arabic Scholars would regard him as an authority in native world of medicine.

AGE OF CHARAKA SANHITA

Though the age of Charaka is mostly believed just before 175 B.C., Charaka Sanhita is believed to have been composed 7-8century B.C by Agni Vesa containing the teaching of Attreya his teacher and the same was revised by Charaka around 175 B.C., including therein new treatments and Ayurvedic recipes.

SUBJECT MATTER OF CHARAKA SANHITA

The Charaka Sanhita is a vast treatise, which describes the various categories of physicians, the code of conduct for medical students and ayurvedic physicians, centres of medical learning, fundamental basics of medical botany etc. As regards the medicine, Charaka describes in detail foetal generation, anatomy of human body, physiology, the three humours of the body, diagnosis, treatment of various diseases etc.

SYSTEM OF MEDICAL EDUCATION

Charaka Sanhita gives vivid idea about the system of medical education being followed in that period. A person aspiring to learn Ayurvedic medicines should approach a teacher of his choice for the purpose and later after having being satisfied regarding the aptitude, social and physical biodata, would allow him to become his student. Normally the three twice born castes were allowed i.e. Brahmna, Kshatriya, Vaisha were ordained to study medicine. A religious ritual was performed for initiating the student and it consisted of prayer and worshiping the Gods and offering fire sacrifice in presence of teacher and other people. Thereafter a medical oath was taken before the sacred fire.

The contents of medical oath were as under:-

I. *That student will lead the life of bramacharya and speak truth and will take pure articles of food.*

II. *Total dedication to his teacher.*

III. *He shall sincerely work for the relief of patient even for the sake of his life and shall not commit adultry and shall speak, and clean, gentle, pure religious conduct with appropriate behaviour.*

IV. *He shall not treat the person of wicked and miserable character.*

V. *He shall not accept any gift from a woman without the consent of his husband or guardian.*

VI. *The customs of patient's home shall not be made public.*

VII. *With a view to avoid shock to a patient and others, he will not mention that patient was likely to die even if it was so.*

As there was no medical college, neither classrooms nor laboratories were provided in those days, medical education was imparted through apprenticeship method. The student would serve the teacher and watch him treating patients and assist him in making medicines. In this process he may come across the use of various equipments, surgical instruments and other medical procedures. The theoretical and practical training was given by teacher himself. After serving his teacher for several years and teacher having being satisfied with the proficiency and fitness of his pupil, a test to the discretion of teacher was given and then only he was recommended to practice medicines.

CHARAKA'S ANATOMY AND PHYSIOLOGY

Charaka has described the anatomy of human body not much in depth. According to him, human body consists of 360 bones whereas Susurta mentions the number of bones as 300.

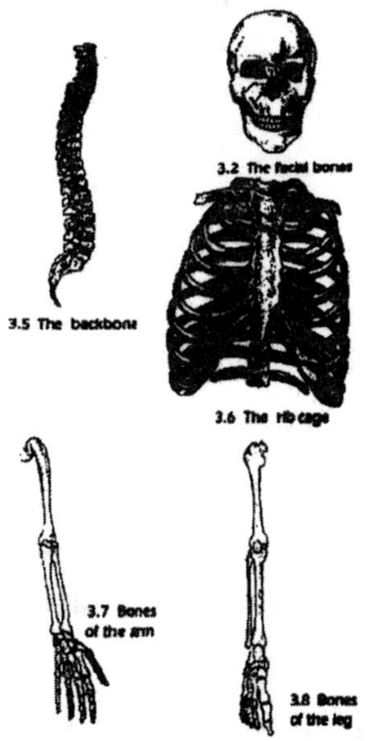

3.2 The facial bones

3.5 The backbone

3.6 The ribcage

3.7 Bones of the arm

3.8 Bones of the leg

As per Charaka, 360 bones include teeth and sockets of teeth each being 32, nails, phallinges, long bones, their bases, heels, ankel bones, wrist bones, bones of forearms, legs, kneecaps, elbow pexs, thighs, arms, shoulder blades, collar bones, hip blades, backbone, chest, ribs, cubercalyx, neck bone, windpipe, cavities, bones of jaw, nose, cheeks, burrows and temple etc. The description of heart, muscles, brain, lungs also figures, but in a very cursory manner.

The physiology of Charaka is based upon Ayurvedic conceptions and accordingly human body as well as the food stuff composed of five elements namely earth, fire, water, wind and either etc. They stand for solid, liquid, gas, energy and either.

THREE AYURVEDIC HUMOURS

The three humours of Ayurveda namely wind, bile, phlegm have very important functions in the body. The inhale and exhale of breath speech throwing out of urine faeces and also to give energy are the functions of wind, whereas bile provides heat to the body and helps in digestion. Role of phlegm is to govern weight, power, strength and normal oil to the body. The equilibrium of three dosas or humours is important in maintaining normal health of a person. Disease occurs when one or more of them predominated in the body.

DIAGNOSIS

Before the treatment is prescribed, Charaka Sanhita emphasizes the diagnosis of the disease and proper and thorough examination of patient is necessary for the purpose. The physician must go in the cause of disease, its symptoms, the constitution and age of the patient, his vitality and all other relevant factors in this regard. Not only he should prescribe the medicines but the diet and proper lifestyle should also be advised to enable the patient for speedy cure.

KINDS OF DISEASES AND THEIR CAUSES:-

Charaka has given a detailed description of various diseases including of eyes and specific diseases of females and of children. The diseases are caused due to predominance of any of three humours or may be accidental, violent or mild and may also be caused by demons. Taking improper diet, excessive or faulty exposure of senses and other conditions adversely effect the three humours i.e. wind, bile and phelgm leading to spoiled equilibrium and reacting upon various Dhatus of body.

GENERATION & DEVELOPMENT OF FOETUS:-

This has been described in vast detail. Determination of sex before birth has also been mentioned. Indication for male child had been mentioned as under:

I. Detection of milk in right breast.

II. Desire for company of female by the mother

III. Bulging of abdomen due to foetus on right side

IV. Male like temperament and actions

V. Longing or desire for things with a male name

VI. Raising right foot while walking

INDICATION FOR FEMALE CHILD

Vice versa indications will be evinced by mother in case of female child.

CHARAKA'S DRUGS:-

Mainly vegetable products and earth products have been classified into 50 groups. Various forms of drugs such as powder, pill, convection permanted, medicated oils or ghee, inhalers as well as injections into rectum, uretara etc. have been described. In nutshell the Charaka Sanhita is comprised of Ayurvedic medicines & treatment. It even prescribes status of physicians, their fee, nursing care and schools of medical learning, medical botany, various customs, traditions, habits of smoking and drinking of the period.

CHARKA

An Ayurvedic Physician

AT A GLANCE

Important Works

- *Charka sanhita(revised version)*

Achievements

- *Given new treatments and ayurvedic recipies.*
- *Prescribed the System of medical education*

17

Patanjali
A Pioneer of Science of Yoga

17

PATANJALI
A PIONEER OF SCIENCE OF YOGA

Patanjali, the great expounder of Yoga, is still remem bered by millions of people all over the world irrespective of caste and creed. His *Yoga-Sutra* is one of the monumental work on Yoga practice. In some of the ancient Indian literature Patanjali has been identified with, and in others distinguished from his namesake who composed *Mahabhashya,* the great commentary on *Paniniyam.* Legends describe him as an incarnation of Sesha, the serpent king. Pataniali is believed to have lived in second century BC.

AIM OF YOGA

The term "Yoga" means union which connects the mortal to Supreme God. The *YogaSutra* in its second aphorism, describes yoga as the 'inhibition of the modification of the mind'. Mind is like a pond agitated by waves of thoughts, hence its control is necessary to attain God.

STAGES OF YOGA

To attain oneness with God, Yoga suggests certain physical and mental disciplines which is divided into eight successive stages, hence it is also called "Astanga-Yoga". These eight stages are *vama, nijyama, vairagya, asana,*

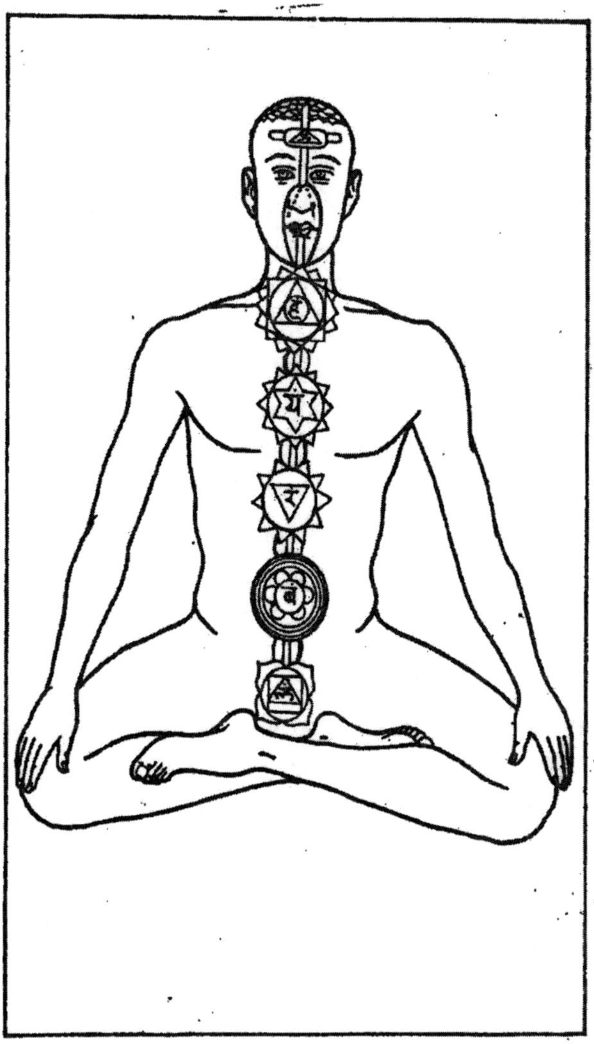

Seven Chakras

pranayama, pratyahara, dharana and *dhvana* which in turn leads to the great final stage of *samadhi* in which the yogi overcomes time and space.

WHAT IS YOGA

The theory of Yoga says that "man is the microcosm, world is macrocosm", which means within man's corporeal frame embraces all the subtle planes of the universe; beyond his physical existence there is a parallel 'etheric-double' which constitutes his subtle body. The subtle envelopes are related to the gross body at several psychic points. The numerous etheric channels are known as *nadis,* and of them the most important ones are the *Ida* or lunar channel *(Chandra—nadi)* and the *Pingala* or Solar channel *(Surya—nadi)* which run upwards towards the nose respectively along the right and left side of the central subtle channel called the *S'ushumna-nadi* that runs through the central channel of the spinal column.

There are also a series of seven *Chakras* (centres) situated along the spinal column whose locations are as follows: the *Muladhar Chakra* at the base of the spinal column between the anal orifice and the sacral plexus; *Svadishtana Chakra* at the base of the genital organ *Manipuraka* near the navel; *Anahata* near the heart; *Visuddha* at the juncture of the spinal column and medulla oblongata, behind the throat; *Ajna* between the eyebrows and finally *Sahasrara* located about four finger-breadths above the crown of the head; it is also called *Brahmarandhra* and is the meeting-place of the *Kundalini Sakti* with Pure Consciousness.

The *Kundalini* is the microcosmic form of universal energy which is described as lying 'coiled', inactive' or in 'trance sleep' at the base of the spine, technically called the *Muladhara Chakra,* blocking the opening of the *Sushumna* that leads to the *Sahasrara Chakra* in the brain centre. By performing *Pranayama* in scientific way, one send the current impulses to strike at the root impulses of *Kundalini* to awaken it. Once it wakes up, then in the successive stages of yoga, this energy rises up step by step through the *Sushumna-nadi* and the various *Chakras* along the spinal column and goes up to the centre in the head *(Brahmarandhra,).* When this happens, the yogi attains illumination and he becomes one with God. This is the union of *Atma* and *Paramatma.*

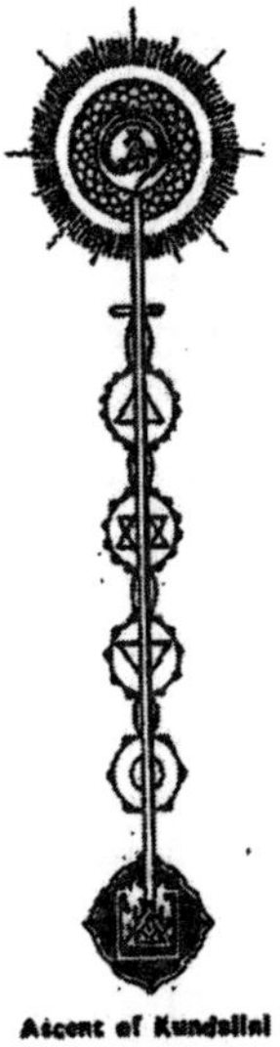

Ascent of Kundalini

MIRACLES OF YOGA

The power of Yoga is immense which can yield both spiritual and temporal wealth according to the wish of the Sadhaka (aspirant). It can cure different types of disorders of the body and mind. On the one hand it helps an ardent Sadhaka to attain Moksha on the other it leads to an ordinary householder to a healthy worldly life.

By practicing yoga, says Patanjali, one attains supernatural powers known as Siddhis. However, such Siddhis are considered to be the indirect result of this practice, the attainment of which should not be the ultimate aim of an ardent Yogi. This is because if a Sadhaka gets entangled himself by such Siddhis he will not be able to attain Mokhsha.

An Autobiography of a Yogi of great saint Shri Paramahamsa Yogananda narrates in its foreword that even after the *mahasauzadhi* (death) of the saint his body did not show any sign of deterioration for weeks. Swami Vivekananda says even the heart can be made to stop or go on at yogi's bidding. Some of the great yogis like Sri Ramakrishna Paramahamsa and Sri Shirdi Sai Baba have been witnessed to stop the beating of their hearts and to hold breath completely for weeks. Curiously, many times they were confirmed dead by the doctors.

Kundalini's rising, in the language of modern science, means the activation of the vast dormant areas of the brain many Universities in the world have incorporated Yoga in their curriculum. Yoga has great importance in the modern world of stress and restlessness. It also helps carry out research in parapshychology, and metaphysics.

PATANJALI

Founder of Science of Yoga

Age And Birth

Age 2nd century B.C.

Important Works

- *Yogsutra of Patanjali on yoga practice*

Achievements

- Unfolded the power of yoga
- Expounder of kundalni shakti and various chakras.
- Awakening of kundalni.

18

Kapila

Founder of Sankhya Philosophy of Creation of the Universe

18

KAPILA FOUNDER OF SANKHYA PHILOSOPHY OF CREATION OF THE UNIVERSE

The authenticity of scientific revelations may be estab lished or rejected from time to time with the new experiments and discoveries. It is at this juncture, it would be worthwhile to look into the theory of cosmogenesis promulgated by the Sankhya philosophy of Kapila about 2500 years ago. It reveals how far the modern science shares the views of the Sankhya philosophy of the creation of the Universe.

The Sankhyas argue that Kapila, the founder of the Sankhya system is mentioned in the Svetasvatara Upanishad (V.2) 'it is he, who in the beginning, bears (nourishes) by thoughts Kapila sage when born and looks on while he is being born'. Rishi Kapila, the reddish sage, is also described as the Hiranyagarbha (the golden child).[1] In the *Vishnupurarni* IV. 4. 12 Kapila (Vasudeva) is said to a part of Bhagavan Purushottama, who reduced to ashes the 60 thousand sons of Sagara, on the suspicion that the Asvamedha horse grazing

1. Vedntasutra of Badarayana (II.I.1) with Sankarabhashya

near that sage had been stolen by him. The story is also mentioned in *Vanaparva* 47(7-18) of Mahabharata. In RigVeda X.27.16 Kapila is mentioned as one among ten Angirases. In *Vanapan'a* (221 .26) Kapila is mentioned as promulgator of Sankhya-Yoga. The *Vainana Puran* (60.70) mentions Kapila as the knower of Sankhya. Kapila is also said to be the 50fl of Vithata and Devahuti, and a descendant of the great Brahman sage, Manu, the law-giver. He was probably born at Pushkara, a sacred bathing place near modern Ajmer and lived at Ganganagar in eighth or seventh century BC. However Kapila stands a legendary figure as nothing much is known about his life. There are much controversial aspects regarding the life time of Kapila. Being the propounder of Sankhya philosophy, he was. during the later period attached with so many legends and epithets such as "the son of the Brahma", "the incarnation of Vishnu", "a form of Agni", etc.

The origin of the Sankhya philosophy is still a matter of debate. Chinese sources say that there were eighteen Sankhya schools. Scholars are of different opinions regarding the meaning of the word Sankhya and its application to the system of philosophy which it represents. According to one school 'Sankhya' means 'number', hence enumeration. They held that as the Sankhya system enumerated twenty-five tattvas it is likely that the philosophy came to be called Sankhya. Finding etymological root of the word Sankhya, Bhagavad Datta says Sankhya means science. Amarakosa mentions

---

2. Bhagavad Datta. 1968. *The Story of Creation as Seen by the Seers*. Delhi: Itihasa Prakashana Mandala
3. Carcha sankhya vicharana

Sankhya as national examination'.[3] However, majority of people think that by Sankhya is meant perfect knowledge or wisdom.

The history of cosmic evolution, according to Sankhya, is based on the principles of conservation, transformation and dissipation of energy. The cosmos is evolved of an unmanifested ground, called Prakriti, which is conceived to be constituted by three gunas when they are in equilibrium.[4] The three gunas (factors) are sattva the light or intelligence — stuff), *rajas* (the energy — stuff producing motion, force, etc.) and tamas (the matter — stuff which is mass or inertia having coarse, inert, enveloping and dark qualities, offers resistance to opposing).

Evolution begins with the disturbance of this primordial balance of three gunas by the transcendental or magnetic influence of Purusha, the Universe of Consciousness. The equilibrium of Prakriti is thus disturbed by the Purusha. Disequilibrium breaks up the uniform diffusion and impels the aggregation of the gunas to a state in which one or more is relatively preponderant over the others, a creative transformation accompanied by evolution of motion. Thus, these three gunas combine in various proportions and make up the evolving universe.

STAGES OF CREATION

From Prakrti evolves mahan (i.e. buddhi, consciousness) from which arises ahankara, from which evolve on the one

4. Sattvarajstamasam samyavastha

hand the five tanmatras (subtle elements, viz. sabda, sparsa, gaudha. rasa, rupa) and on the other hand, manas (mind) and the ten indriyas (sense-organs). From the live subtle elements are evolved the five great elements- earth, water, tejas. Vayu and akasa (ether). Differentiation of the great elements are themselves complex Tanmatric structures and their formation occurred as follows. Akasa (Ether) was produced by the aggregation of sabda tanmstras, Vayu by the combination of sabda and sparsa, Fire by rupa. sabda and sparsa, water by rasa, sabda, sparsa and rupa, earth by gandha. sabda, sparsa, rupa and rasa. The vast variety of substances, composed only of five Bhutas (pancha bhiitas), are the result of the differences in the attachment of various Gunas and Tanmatras in them. Thus trigunas are very important in the formation of various objects.

These three Gunas are instable as they are always uniting, separating and uniting again leading to the two-fold processes of creation and destruction. Though in combination Gunas form various objects, they themselves can neither be created nor be destroyed. In the processes of creation of the universe, the successive changes occur not from whole to parts or from parts to whole, but from a relatively less coherent, less determinate whole to a relatively more coherent, more determinate, more differentiated whole.

---

1. पृथ्वी अप् तेजः वायु आकाश़ः

COMPARISON WITH MODERN THEORIES

Even though the modern science boasts of reaching the distant planets yet the truth of creation of the matter and the universe remains a polemic problem for it. However, the theories of creation of the Universe postulated by some of the prominent scientists of the world go with the theories promulgated by the Sankhya philosophy. The Sankhya doctrine postulates that in the process of evolution, matter and mind evolved concurrently from the original hub of energy. In a physicalistic attempt to link matter and mind, an eminent astronomer, V.A. Firsoff, postulates the existence of extremely subtle particles of mind stuff, or mindons, of a quasi-ethereal quality. He suggests that mind is 'a universal entity or interaction of the same order as electricity or gravitation, and that there must exist a *modulus of transformation,* analogous to Einstein's famous equality $E = mc^2$. According to Professor Hoyle "material does not come from anywhere, but it simply appears". In the opinion of Professor Bondi and Sir Harold Spencer Jones "the creation is out of nothing". Prof. J.R. Oppenheimer on the other hand says, "The new particles come out of the universal primordial matrix of quiescent energy". His "universal primordial matrix of quiescent energy" has parallels in the Prakrti of Kapila's Sankhya Philosophy.

The ancient Hindu scientists used both empirical and intuitive disciplines which helped them go into the known to the realm of the unknown to unravel the mysteries of the universe. Thus, metaphysics may provide working hypotheses for some of the enigmatic problems of modern science.

19

Varamihra
Newton of Gupta Age

19

VARAMIHRA
NEWTON OF GUPTA AGE

Varamihra was not only a great astronomer but was a scientist also. His work Punchsidhanta is considered to be the historical literature of Indian astronomical science. After the Vedic age there was a trend to study the horizon and the other contemporary developments resulting into exchange of views between Greek & India regarding astronomy and Varmihra is the astronomical scientist of this age. He was born towards the end of 5th century in Ujjain which was a part of Magadh empire (Madhya Bharat) in those days and was a son of Brahman Aditya Das. Varahmihra is the author of many works of astronomy and astrology and many of his books are still not available. All of his works could be divided into three parts:

i) Astronomy

ii) Astrology

iii) Agriculture.

Panchasiddhantika is the most outstanding work of Varahmihra which deals with 5 systems of astronomy as under :

i) Paitamaha

ii) Saurya

iii) Romaka

iv) Paulisa and

v) Vasistha Siddhantas

Out of which he assigns the first place to Saurya Sidshanta. As regards the Paitamaha Siddhantas though it attempts to lead to the prediction of solar eclipses but has been incapable of furnishing any rule to that end like other Indian astronomers.

Among five systems of astronomy described in Panchasiddhantika, the full text of treatise of only Saurya Siddhanta is available to us presently. The modern Saurya Siddhanta is very much the same in fundamental features as mentioned by Varahamihra. A cursory review of those chapters of the Panchasiddhantika treatise of the Saurya Siddhanta show at once that the treatise of the same known to Varamihra agreed with the modern Saurya Siddhanta. The methods of the two treatises are essentially the same and on the other hand sufficiently different from those of the other Siddhanta summarized by Varmihara to ensure the Saurya Siddhanta in its twofold form a distinct position of its own. But it must also be taken into account that the two treatises (the old we possess today) are different in many assential points and details. For example, the old Saurya Siddhanta assigned the mean diameters of the Sun and Moon the values 32'5" and 30'54" (Psi.IX.15-16) while according to the modern, the corresponding values are 32' 3.6" and 32' respectively.

There are other differences also between two Saurya Siddhanta in regard to the number of the years in a Maha Yuga, number of inter Calari months and omitted lunar days. Maha Yuga according to Varamihra will consist of twenty eight days less than that of modern Saurya Siddhanta days. Further there is a difference in respect to the mean revolution of the planets.

As regards Paitamaha Siddhanta, there is a small chapter devoted to the system in Panchasiddhantika and the five stanzas quoted in the chapter make clear the important substance of the siddhanta. The perusal of which shows that the siddhanta belongs to the same category as the Jyautisa Vedanga. and the Garga Samhita and it could be identified with them. According to which the Yuga contains sixty solar months, sixty two symbolical months etc.

According to the teaching of Pitamaha, five years constitute a Yuga of Sun and Moon. The adhimasas are brought about by thirty months and an omitted lunar day (avama) by sixty-two days.

Lessen the time of the Saka king by two, and divide by five; with the remaining years from the ahargana, which begins with the bright-half of Magha. The ahargana begins with the day, viz, from sunrise.

In the quinquennial luni-solar yuga of the Paitamaha Siddhanta, one adhimasa is comprised within each period of thirty solar months and one Avama, i.e. omitted lunar day within each of sixty two days.

According to this Stanza which directs us to deduct two from the number of elapsed Saka year, a new yuga began with 2 Saka elapsed.

If the ahargana is increased by its own sixty-first part, the result are the tithis. If it is multiplied by nine and divided by 122, the result is the namsatra of the Sun. Multiply the ahargana by 7, divide by 610 and deduct (the result from the ahargana), the result is the lunar maksatra, counting from Dhanistha.

REVOLVING OF EARTH

Varamihra regarded earth as an immovable sphere fixed at the centre of the universe around which the Sun, Moon and other planets revolved. A bird would not return to its nest as soon as it had flown away from it, had there been any motion in the earth. However, the modern astronomy has proved that the fact is otherwise. Regarding the position of the things on earth and its power he says that mountains, rivers, trees cities, men and angees all are around the globe of the earth and two cities are opposite to each other, it is difficult to say one is low in relation to the other. How can one say that one place of the earth is low as it is in every particular identical with another place of earth and one place could be as little flat as any other.

Varamihra has also written about astrology and Vrihat Jataka is the treatise on the subject which is still available but the subject of the work is limited to Horoscopy Astrology.

VARAMIHRA AS AN AGRONOMIST

This is yet another aspect of versatility of Varamihra. A section of his work Vrihat Samhita is devoted to the method

for making the soil soft and suitable for sowing seeds or planting saplings. Varamihra described the method for better flowering and fruit formation as well as for the planting of saplings. and he suggested that the plant sapling should be first given bath in water. Various constellations in the sky are mentioned under whose influence the planting of the saplings leads to their better flourishing. The saplings whose branches and leaves are not yet developed are recommended to be planted in the months of January and February, those with just developed branches in the months of November and December and the ones with well developed branches in the months of June and July. Names are given of the trees which ought to be propagated by means of their cuttings. Grafting is described to be a better method which is done either by inserting the cutting of a plant on the roots or the stem of another plant. Cuttings and grafts are smeared over with cowdung. For transplanting, the plants are smeared over from root to top with clarified butter(ghee), Appropriate distance is left between two plants so that their roots do not intermingle because that leads to their ill functioning and the trees do not bear fruits. After planting, the trees are watered in the morning and evening in the summer, at the end of the day in winter and during the rainy season only when the earth is dry. Trees like Azadirachta (nim) are mentioned to be conducive to the welfare of the house if planted in residential places.

DISEASES IN TREES

Varamihra has also suggested treatment to avoid diseases in trees resulting into non-development of the buds, dry branches and yellow leaves etc. As a general prophylactic measure against such exigencies, mud kneaded with ghee and vidanga is recommended to be applied to the roots and diluted milk poured around them. Varamihra says that a good growth of plants in a dry area indicates the presence of water under the soil.

It will thus be seen that Varamihra was a scientist who has dealt with various subjects like astronomy, astrology, agriculture, revolving of earth etc. He has mentioned various subjects on astronomy to know the divisions of time, ages, years, seasons, months, muhurtas, vipalas etc. as dealt by him in 5 siddhantas. While it is a fact that Varamihra's writing were influenced by Greek astronomy, his contribution is significant to the science of astrology though some of his views were either not correct as in many of his writings traditional views are reflected. In view of the religious and social environment prevailing in those days it will be uncharitable to blame him for his views and in the words of Alberuni "On the whole, his foot stands firmly on the basis of truth and he clearly calls out the truth".

VARAMIHRA

AT A GLANCE

Age And Birth

Born in Ujjain- ending 5th Century A.D

Important Works

- *Punh Ka Sithanta- the most outstanding work*
- *Astrology and Vrihatjatka*

Contribution

- *Expounded five systems of astronomy.*
- *Astrology.*
- *Agronomy.*

20

Arya Bhata

The Founder of Algebra

20

ARYA BHATA
THE FOUNDER OF ALGEBRA

"Aryabhata is the master who, after reaching the farthest shores and plumbing the inmost depths of the sea of ultimate knowlege of mathematics, kinematics and spherics, handed over the three sciences to the learned world".

Commentary on Aryabhatiya
by Bhaskara I

Aryabhatta was the first algebraist of ancient India and whatever he expounded was entirely his own contribution. After Vedanga-Jautisa where we have a glimpse of arithmeatic and algebra, supposed to be a work of 700 B.C., there has been a gap of nearly 700 years in Indian astronomy. Aryabhatta was a real astronomer and mathematician appeared in ancient

Indian horizon making a significant contribution in the new science known as algebra.

Ayrabhatta was born in 476 A.D. and is famous by his treatise Aryabhatiya which is a composition of 499 A.D. Though nothing is very clear about his birth place but the treatise which is a land mark in the field of science of algebra was composed in Kusumapura near Patna, Bihar.

TWO ARYABHATTAS

There have been two persons of same name as Aryabhatta and the great algebraist and scientist is Aryabhatt-I who wrote two treatise one at the age of 23 and another at an advance stage, only the later is available to us. What is more remarkable in the treatise is that the yuga supposed to begin from mid-night and the number of savana days in a Mahayuga exceeded by 300, though in the first treatise Yuga has been described to begin from the sunrise.

The treatise Aryabhattya is divided into 4 chapters called Padas. The first is called Gitika Pada (ii) Ganita Pada (iii) Kalakriya Pada (iv) Go a Pada. The first part containg 11 verses is the smallest chapter and only described the fruit of the study of these verses.

The most important chapter is the Ganita Pada which contains 33 verses, the subjects dealt with are squares, cubes, square root, cube root, area of a triangle and volume of a prism, area of a circle and volume of a sphere, area of a quadrilateral, circumference of a circle Rsine, determination of the Rsine of the zenith distance, the base of a right angled triangle and the upright of a right angled triangle, reversed sine, areas of circular figures, rule of three, reduction of fractions, inverse rule of three, evaluation of unknown values, and the theory of pulveriser.

The Kalakriya Pada containing only 23 verses deals with the units of time e.g. 12 months constitute one year, 30 days – one month, 60 nadi – one day, and 60 vinadis are equall to 24 minutes, the time taken by a normal man in having 6 breaths constitutes 24 seconds etc.

The Gola Pada deals with the Sun's path, the ascending nodes of planets and the shadow of the Earth etc.

Contribution of Aryabhatta to the Science of Algebra, Astronomy and Geometry :

Foundation of Algebra laid – In the science of algebra Arya Bhatta gave the solution of many a problems of mathematics and also made new observation in geometry. The solution of the quadratic equation in algebra which was undetreminate first degree equation containing X^1 with value of X not obtainable in integral term was for the first time given by him, which is correct. The value of $\pi = 3.1416$ was obtained correct to the four places of decimal. The time of calculation of solar eclipse was the problem of astonomers which was solved by Arya Bhatta.

Quadratic Equation : This equation is applied to determine the interest in a problem quoted by Arya Bhatta. An amount of money loaned on unknown interest for six months and the interest is again loaned for a period and all together become Rs. 60. Arya Bhatta gives the solutions of the problem in a verse.

He also provided the solution of simultaneous type quardratic equation in a verse.

A notable achievement of Arya Bhatta was to give the concept of pulveriser and a process has been mentioned by him solving the same which is called Kutta and by this process he is perhaps the first in the history of mathematics in this regard and indeterminate equation of first degree could be solved by this process.

LINEAR EQUATIONS :

A linear equation in algebra in determining some unknown point in one of his verse is translated as under : The difference of the known "amount" relating to two persons should be divided by the difference of the coefficients of the unknown. The quotient will be the value of the unknown, if their possessions are equal.

All this show that a significant and outstanding contribution has been made by Arya Bhatta in the science of Algebra and infact he laid the foundation of Algebra in India.

GEOMETRY AND TRIGONOMETRY

The attainment of Arya Bhatta in Geometry and Trigonometry is marvelous where he has given various methods of solving following geometrical problems :

- Area of the triangle
- Area of the circle
- Circumference of the circle

- Volume of the sphere
- Value of π
- Method of Rsine

Aryabhatta gave a method of measuring the dimension of the shadow thrown by an object placed in part of light and this forming the basis of calculating the eclipse. Pythagaurian theorem was also described by him in one of his verses.

NOTATION OF NUMBERS

He devised a way of denoting of expressing the high number in measurement and used the stopped congonents to represent the nos. 1-25 when they preceded the vowel and high decimal powers of these numbers when they preceded other vowels as under :

a	1
i	100
u	100^2 or 10,000
r	100^3 or 1,000,000
lr	100^4 or 100,000,000
e	100^5 or 10,000,000,000
ai	100^6 or 1,000,000,000,000
o	100^7 or 100,000,000,000,000
au	100^8 or 10,000,000,000,000,000

The units, hundreds, ten thousands, one million etc., with odd placings are known as the vargasthana or the square positions, and tens, thousands, hundred thousands etc., with even number of digits are known as the average-sthana or the nonsquare positions. The India ancient system of digital counting in fact goes upto 10^{22} where in the count proceeds from 10^{16} das kharan to 10^{18} das padam, 10^{20} das neel and finally 10^{22} das padam.

ASTRONOMY

Arya Bhatta discarded the old views and made his own observations in the field of Astronomy. He threw to winds the belief that earth is static and anounced that the earth is a sphere rotating on its axis. Arya Bhatta developed the theory of epicycles to represent the motion of planet. He is the first to declare that lunar and solar eclipses are not caused by Rahu but by the shadow of earth on moon. He made it clear that moon is not self illuminated but it is dark and illuminated by Sun. He devised the method to predict the lunar and solar eclipses.

THE WORD 'SCIENCE' ORIGINATED FROM ARYA BHATTA

According to Amartya Sen-Noble laureate Arya Bhatta has named trigonometry "Jiya Ardha, from which the Arab word "Jeb" is derived. Later on Italian translated this to "Synous" from which the English word Science is derived.

(Reference Address by Prof. Amartya Sen - the Noble Prize winner at the Planery session of the Parvasi Bhartiya Divas celebration on 6th Jan. 2003)

In nutshell, Arya Bhatta is considered to be one of the greatest scientists of ancient India and algebraist par excellence. He is the first ancient mathematician to have made so significant contribution in the field of mathematics of algebra. Solution of indeterminate equation is one of the land marks to the credit of Arya Bhatta. Infact he is one of the most original scientists. He completely contradicted the orthodox view in the field of Astronomy to declare that the eclipses are not caused by Rahu but the shadow of moon on the earth and he was opposed bitterly by the contemporary as well as the mathematicians, astronomers of later times. The modern astronomy has vindicated his views.

ORIGINAL TEXT LOST

"I have not been able to find any thing of the books of Arya Bhatta"

— Alberuni

"A long and diligence search failed to recover the aliphatic and other works of Arya Bhata"

— Cole Brook

It is unfortunate that like many other ancient Indian scientists the original text of Arya Bhatta has been untraceable.

However, a text Arya Bhatiya was compiled later on and published in the year 1784 and it is on the basis of this book that the scientific genius of Arya Bhatta is known and his doctrine and treatise were made public.

ARYABHATA

Age And Birth

Born in 476 A.D. at Ashmaka in the Indian state of Kerala.

Achievements

- Heliocentric theory of gravitation
- One of the earliest persons to support the theory that earth is sphere.
- First to declare that Earth rotates around the Sun, not the Sun around the Earth.
- First to declare that Eclipses are not caused by Rahu or Ketu;but by the shadow of Earth on Moon.

Important Works

- *Main work is known as Aryabhattiya*

21

Brahamgupta
A Great Mathematician

21

BRAHMA GUPTA
A GREAT MATHEMATICIAN

1. $0 - 1 = -1$
2. $1 - 0 = 1$
3. $0 \times 0 = 0$
4. Any quantity $\times 0 = 0$
5. $0 \div 0 = 0$

(Not correct)

Brahma Gupta, according to Albruni – An Arab traveller who visited India around 1100 A.D, had been the most distinguished mathematician of ancient India. He was born in 598 A.D. in the town at Bhillamala near Multan, now in Pakistan. This was the period when the scientific activities were on the declining side on account of disturbed political situation in India.

There are two famous works attributed to Brahma Gupta-

(i) **Brahma's Sphuta Sidhanta** which he wrote when he was thirty years of age under the patronage of King Vyaghra Mukha of Chapa dynasty and is based upon his earlier work Pitamaha Sidhanta which had become outdated. What is remarkable is that in Sphutic Sidhanta, he has given his own independent views and latest knowledge in the subjects of Algebra, geometry, and astronomy and a comparison has been made with the views of other mathematicians as well as Hindu religious scriptures.

(ii) Karan Khanda Khadyaka is another work of Brahma Gupta which is believed to have been written in the year 665 A.D.

CONTRIBUTION OF BRAHMA GUPTA

Algebra – The most notable achievement of Brahma Gupta in the science of Algebra is the concept of zero - showing various aphorism with zero, like zero subtracted from a negative quantity will give negative, if subtracted from positive will give positive. Similarly zero multiplied by zero will give zero, if multiplied by any quantity will also give zero. But zero divided by zero according to him is also zero, which is wrong, as it will be an indeterminate quantity.

SOLUTION OF QUADRATIC EQUATION

Brahma Gupta had very high knowledge of algebra and gave simple rules for solving all types of simple quadratic equations. What is outstanding to his credit is giving the solution of indeterminate second-degree equation. The science of Algebra was taken a new height of excellence by him using the same for astronomical calculations.

GEOMETRY

In his book of Sphuta Sidhantha, Brahma Gupta gives the solution of various problems concerned to geometry. eg-solution of right angle triangle, properties of circle quadrilateral etc. He also gives the value of ratio of circumference of circle to its diameter. However, this value is less accurate than that of Arya Bhatta.

CONTRIBUTION IN THE SCIENCE OF ASTRONOMY

In his work of Sphuta Sidhantha, Brahma Gupta gives the methods of calculation of motions of various planets, Moon and Sun eclipses and system of Astronomy. He reiterated the views of Arya Bhatta that the Earth is round in shape. According to him, stars rise and set in different places at different times on account of the fact that Earth was round. A more significant observation of Brahma Gupta was gravitational force of Earth. It was he who for the first time hinted that Earth has attractive force and he attributed it to the nature of Earth to keep things. However he was not correct to say that Earth is stationary and does not rotate, opined by Arya Bhatta. His observation regarding the cause of eclipses was also not correct. He criticized the view of Arya Bhatta that the eclipses are on account of shadow of moon on Earth and not by Rahu. He has been described as the most distinguished astronomer of his times by Albruni. It appears that he has perhaps bowed down to the prevailing orthodox views described in Puranas regarding eclipses and non-rotation of Earth. Brahma Gupta was under the patronage of the king who may be holding the same views as such speaking out his correct views would have been in bad taste and would not have been likable to the King and the then prevailing Brahmin religion which believed in the orthodox astronomical views.

In nut shell the outstanding achievements of Brahma Gupta were- concept of zero, solution of indeterminate second-degree equation in algebra and taking the science of Algebra to new heights by using the same in astronomical calculations.

BRAHMGUPTA

Age And Birth

Born in 598 A.D. near Multan in Punjab

Important Works

- *Brahma-sphuta-Siddhanta Karna Khanda Khadyaka.*

Achievements

- *Gave concept of Zero.*
- *Solution of indeterminate equations of second degree.*
- *Using algebra for astronomical problems.*
- *Described 20 Arithmetical operations*
- *Provided methods of calucation of Moon and Sun eclipses.*
- *Confirmed that the Earth is round*
- *Upheld the orthodox notion about the non rotation of Earth and form of eclipse*

Special Achievement

- Brahmgupta calculated the circumference of Earth as 5,000 yojanas at 7.2 Kilometers per yojana. That's 36,000 kilometers, which is close to modern computation of 40,000 kilometers.

22

Bhaskara

The Great Algebraist and Astronomer

22

BHASKARA - THE GREAT ALGEBRAIST AND ASTRONOMER

In Medieval India when Hindu sciences were showing the sign of decadence, the horizon of mathematics was illuminated by a shining star - Bhaskara, the great mathematician. There have been two personalities in the same name and both being mathematician as under :

1. Bhaskara - I 470 A.D.
2. Bhaskara - II 1142 A.D.

However, it is Bhaskara II who finds a high place amongst astronomers and mathematicians of India and made a valuable contribution in these fields, which inspired many of the astronomers particularly in the science of Algebra.

BIRTH AND AGE OF BHASKARA

'Mathematician son of Mathematician father' is the appropriate description of Bhaskara's family as his father Mahesvara who was his teacher also, was a mathematician. Bhaskara's son was astronomer as well as mathematician and got royal patronage on account of his eminence in mathematics and astronomy. Bhaskara was born at Vijjadavida in Shahya dry Hills which is a part of modern Maharashtra State, in the year 1114 A.D. The family tree of Bhaskara has been given in some of the text as under :

Trivikrama - Bhaskara Bhatta - Govinda - Prabhakara - Manoratha - Mahesvara - Bhaskara - Laksmidhara - Gangadeva.

WORK OF BHASKARA

Bhaskara is the celebrated author of the following treatises which are highly popular even now :

1. The Siddhantasiromani
2. The Marana - Kutuhala

Siddhantasiromani is the most famous one and has four parts and Leelawati is the first, known as Patiganita and contains 278 verses. Though the work is independent one, however, not the original as writing of the earliest scholars Arya Bhatta, Brahama Gupta, Shridhara, form the essential base of the work. The Patiganita deals with the various units of weight & measure and 20 Arithmatic operations i.e. addition, substraction, multiplication, division square, square root, cube and cube root, eight operations of substraction etc. What is more important is the solution of indeterminate equation beside second degree equations etc.

SIDDHANTA-SHIROMANI PART-II

This is known as Biz-gantia and comprises of 230 verses and deals with the concept and negative and positive numerals, negative & positive unknown quantities, rules of subtraction and addition, multiplication & division. The interesting findings are as under :

The square of a positive or a negative quantity is positive, but the square root of a positive quantity could be either positive or negative. The square root of a negative quantity cannot be derived.

UNKNOWN QUANTITY

Bhaskara in his Bijj-Ganita says that unknown quantity can be added or substracted from the one of the same kind not from the different one. In mathematical terms it means that 2a could be added to or substracted from 6a or 8a or 9a but not from 5b or 5c etc. Similarly $5a^3$ could be added or substracted to $3a^3$, $5a^3$, $4a^3$ and so on. He also mentioned as to how unknown quantity could be represented and he suggested that the name of colours like kalka, Pataka, Vahitaka should be used for the purpose. Bhaskara also made considerable progress in every abbreviated notation and instead of using entire word he has stipulated a method of writing device to donate a division of a quantity by an another quantity.

BHASKARA'S ASTRONOMY

The subject of astronomy has been dealt in his treastise of Ganita Adhyaya and Gola Adhyaya of Siddhanta Shiromani, Bhaskara attributed the motion of the planets to weather which he derived from atmospheric currents. He developed a theory to analyse the motion of Sun. Bhaskara's astronomy is more or less based upon Surya Siddhanta.

POPULARITY OF BHASKARA'S TREATISES

The treatises of Bhaskara are highly popular as number of commentaries were written on them. His work Leelawati was translated under the title "Algebra with Arithmatic of Braham Gupta and Bhaskara in the year 1817 by H.T. Colebrood. An English version of Leelawati was done by J. Tylore in the year 1816. Similarly Bhaskara's Bij-Ganita was also translated in London in the year 1817.

Akbar the great Mugal got the Leelawati and Bijja-Ganita translated into Persian in the year 1578 and 1634 A.D. respectively. In nutshell Bhaskara's contribution to arithmatic and algebra is significant and will also be remembered.

CONCEPTION OF ZERO

As regards Bhaskara, the statement of zero more or less appears to be based upon Brahama Gupta. He says that zero added or subtracted from a quantity does not change a number. Also the product will be zero if any quantity is multiplied by zero or zero multiplied by any quantity. Similarly zero divided by any quantity could furnish zero. He however, corrected the conception of Brahama Gupta when he says that any quantity divided by zero would be determinate infinite. To an infinite quantity if any thing is added or substracted, it will remain infinite without causing any material difference.

BHASKARA

AT A GLANCE

Age And Birth

Born in the year 1114 A.D. at Vijjadavida a part of modern Maharashtra state.

Important Works

- *The Sidddhantasiromani*
- *The Marana-Kutuhala*

Achievements

- *Significant contribution to arithmetic and algebra.*
- *Reiterated the concept of zero and corrected the misconception of Brahmgupta.*

23

Vag Bhata

A Great Physician

23

VAG BHATA
A GREAT PHYSICIAN

Vagbhata is a great medical authority of ancient India, and is known through his monumental works Ashtanga Sangralia and Ashtanga Hrudaya Sahita, still considered authorative by Ayurvedic Physicians all over India.

AGE AND BIRTH OF VAGBHATA

Ashtanga Sangraha and Ashtanga Hrudaya mention Vagbhata, the son of Simhagupta, was born in the country of Sindhu, the area around the course of river Indus. He studied under a Buddhist teacher named Avalokita. It is believed that Vagbhata, though a Vedic Brahman by birth, was influenced considerably by the teachings of Gautama Buddha and later in life adopted Buddhism as his religion. However, various passages from Ashtanga Hrudaya show strong Vedic influence on his work. Tibetan, Chinese and Arabian sources support the view that Vagbhata flourished somewhere between the end of the sixth and the beginning of the seventh centuries AD.

There is much debate regarding Vagbhata and his works. Vagbhata is said to have written two medical treatises namely Ashtanga Sangraha (summary of the Octopartite Science) and Ashtanga Hrudaya Samhita (Heart or Essence of the Octopartite Science). However, some of the modern scholars feel that there were two Vagbhatas. They state that Ashtanga Hrudaya was based on an earlier treatise namely Ashtanga Sangraha whose author was another older Vagbhata. Those who support the former theory beleive that the Ashtanga Hrudaya was composed by the same author of the Ashtanga Sangraha when he was much older, more experienced and capable of framing his own views instead of totally depending on the earlier writers. However, at present there seems to be no indisputable and adequate evidence to suggest that there were two different Vagbhatas as authors of the above two medical treatises.

WORKS OF VAGBHATA

ASHTANGA SANGRAHA

Ashtanga Sangraha is composed in a combination of verse and prose form. It is divided into six sections having total 150 chapters. The first section on the Practice of Medicine describes the initiation of the students, longevity and the methods of attaining it, daily and seasonal observances, origin of diseases, properties of different food articles such as rice, meat, herbs, fruits, characteristics of poisoned food, treatment after having taken poisoned food, precaution to be observed by the kings, incompatibility in the foods, personal hygiene, drugs and their subdivisions, collection, composition, taste, strength, qualities and actions of medicinal substances, emetic and astringent drugs, three *doshas* namely *vayu, pitta* and *kapha* and their derangement, various diseases, examination of the patient, principles of treatment, snuffs, fumigants, gargles, treatment of eye diseases with soothing applications and eye drops, venesection, extraction of foreign bodies, caustics, cautery and their uses.

Second section describes various aspects regarding human anatomy, pregnancy and child birth. Third section describes causes and pathology of various ailments. Fourth section is on purgation and vomiting. Fifth and the last section describes management of children, causes of diseases of children and their treatment, ailments related to various parts of body and their treatment, treatment of poisoning, snake, insect, spider and mouse bites and the use of aphrodisiacs etc.

HRUDAYA SAMHITA

Ashtanga Hrudaya Samhita, in 120 chapters and divided into six sections, quotes Charaka, Susruta, Bhela, Nimi, Kasyapa, Dhanvantari and other earlier authors and their works. The chief source, however, is Ashtanga Sangraha. The work presents lucid description of the whole of Ayurvedic medicine with special reference to surgery as given in Susruta Samhita. It does not mention the use of opium, pulse feeling and other metallurgical processes.

Ashtanga Sangraha and Ashtanga Hrudaya are still consulted by the modern physicians for preparing Ayurvedic medicines since they are authoritative works like *Sahasrayogam*. Many later writers like Sarangadhara, Chakrapanidatta and Bhavamisra have frequently quoted these two works. Even after thousands of years have left since their compilation, their authenticity and relevance have not been challenged by anybody. This reveals the importance of these great treatises.

VAG BHATA

Age And Birth

Around 6th-7th century A.D, bithplace in the country of Sindhu around river Indus.

Important Works

- *Ashtanga Sangrah, Ashtanga hrudaya Samhita an authorative works on Ayurvedic Medicines.*

24

Bhoja

A Great Ship Design Engineer

24

BHOJA - A GREAT SHIP DESIGN ENGINEER

Indian shipping has long and glorious past and the ancient people were using the vessels in rivers as well as in seas for commercial and maritime activities. The Indian ships would ply far and wide on different routes and seas. Rig Veda which is considered to be the most ancient and authentic work of around 2000 B.C contains a reference of a ship with one hundred oars. There is evidence of commercial shipping earlier to even this period as Indian teak wood has been found in the ruins of Ur and Yul Bagas - the first king of United Baby-Lonia ruled in Ur in 3000 B.C. The kind of teak was identified as belonging to Malabar Coast and must have been sent by sea.

During the period of Maurya, Gupta and Harsh Vardhan, the sea voyages were made to Malaya Peninsula and the colonization of Annam Combodia and Java by Hindus have been possible only through maritime shipping activities.

All these brisk activities in shipping and navigation necessitate a sound base of technology for fabricating boats and ships and there must be designers of ships, craftmen and the other experts relating to the art and science of ship building.

In this context the name of a great ship design engineer named as Bhoja Narpati is worth mentioning.

There are two persons in the name of Bhoja. One has been the king of Dhar of Malwa Kingdom in 11th Century A.D and the other is Bhoja Narpati who appears to be an expert in designing of ships and boats. Yukti-Kalpa is the work of Bhoja Narpati which is an encyclopedia in vessel building. It comprises the designs, the shape and sizes of different vessels and their capacities, the materials used, the cabins in the ship, their furnishing and their location in the ship all have been described elaborately. This shows that Bhoja Narpati has been a great designer and an authority in building ships and boats.

KINDS OF VESSELS ACCORDING TO YUKTI KALPA :

The vessels were classified as under:

Samanya which means simple and ordinary kind mostly plied in rivers.

Visesha which means special vessels. They were strong, steady and were meant for seas for navigation and meri-time activities.

The ordinary kind of vessels had 10 varieties, smallest being 16 x 4 x 4(in cubits) (length x breath x height) 1 cubit = 20.62 inch. The biggest size under ordinary class called Manthra was of the size of 120 x 60 x 60.

The Visesha kind of vessels which were meant for seas were of two classes.

i) **Dirgha** - This means bigger one and had ten varieties. The largest size being 176 x 22 x 17 (dimension in cubits)

ii) **Unnata** class of vessel were of advanced kind and were perhaps costlier having five varieties the biggest size was 96 x 48 x 48.

CABIN

The ships mentioned above were having cabins inside them and the location of cabins inside the ships would depend upon the purpose for which they were to be used. The vessels meant for naval warfare and long journeys were having cabins towards the front side. The ships having cabins in the middle part were meant for kings and used in pleasure trips.

The ships with location of cabins end to end were of large capacities and meant for transport purpose.

MATERIALS USED-

(i) The main body of vessel was constructed of wood having good marine qualities and should not get rotten in water and not to disintegrate in sea water.

The wood used was also classified on caste basis i.e. Brahmna class, Kshatriya class, Vaishya class and shudra class.

(ii) Cooper, Gold and Silver were used for decorating and furnishing the vessels

The use of iron in the ship was completely avoided as there is a possibility that the magnetic rocks being present in

the sea may influence the ship and its safety may be adversely affected.

COLOUR AND DESIGN OF SHIPS

Interestingly different colours were given to ships depending upon the number of masts with the vessel as under:

I) **Ships with one mast** - **blue colour**

II) **Two mast** - **yellow colour**

III) **Three mast** - **red colour**

IV) **Four mast** - **white colour**

The shape of the front of the ship was like lion, tiger, duck, parrot etc.

In nut shell the eloberate description given in the book Yukti Kalpa on the size, materials, design, technology and all other aspects is a definite evidence that Bhoja Narpati was a great designer of ships and also was aware with the art and science of vessel building in ancient India. There may be other several technicians on ship building on account of which the ancient India was in the forefront in shipping. It is however, unfortunate that in later time, journey by ship was looked down upon with the result that India suffered in commerce and shipping. The situation reached a point that any person travelling by ship and taking sea voyoge was out cast and extricated from the society.

BHOJA

A Great Ship Designer

Age & Birth Controversial

Important Works

- *Ukti-Kalpa, an encyclopedia in vessel designs.*

Achievements

- *Categorized the vessel based upon sizes*
- *Specified the material for building the vessels.*
- *Suggested the colours and designs for ship.*

25

Bibliography

BIBLIOGRAPHY

(In addition to that given in references with every chapter)

Alberuni's Indica (1031A.D.)

Aryabhatiya (1930)

Trans. with notes by Walter Eugene Clark.

Atharvaveda-Samhita (1905)

English Trans. by W.D. Whitney.

Basham A.L. (1954)

The Wonder that was India. Sidgwicd and Jackson, London.

Beal Samuel (1958)

Travels of Hiuen-Tsang Vol. I.

Bentley John (1825)

Historical View of Hindu Astronomy.

Burgess E. (1935)

English translation of the Surya-siddhanta.

Caraka Samhita (1949)

English version.www**Datta B.B. (1932)**

The Science of the Sulbas, Univ. of Calcutta.

Jaggi O.P.

Scientists of Ancient India.

Karambelkar V.W. (1961)

The Atharva Veda and the Ayurveda. Publisher Ku. Usha Karambelkar Tulsi bag Rd., Nagpur.

Kaye G.R. (1924)

Hindu Astronomy.

Keith A.B. (1921)

Indian Logic and Atomism.

Kutumbiah P. (1962)

Ancient Indian Medicine, Orient Longman's Ltd., Madras.

Majumdar R.C. (1952 to 1965)

The History and Culture of the Indian People.

Max Muller (1882)

Heritage of India.

Mishra Umesh (1936)

Conception of Matter. Allahabad.

Mookerji R.K. (1957)

Indian Shipping. 2nd Ed. Longmans, Madras.

Mukhopadhayaya G.N. (1923 to 1926)

History of Indian Medicine 2 vols. Univ. of Calcutta.

Ravi Varma (1940)

Ayurveda and Technical Sciences.

Satya Prakash (1965)

Founders of Sciences in Ancient India. The Research Instt. of Ancient Scientific Studies. New Delhi.

Seal B.N. (1958)

The Positive Sciences of Ancient Hindus.

Susruta Samhita (1907-8)

Trans. into English by Kaviraj Kunja Lal Bhishagaratna, Calcutta.

Zimmer H. (1948)

Hindu Medicine. The Johns Hopkins Press, Baltimore.